What Other

MW01068093

"Two gritty athletes give us a peek behind the curtain to see what it would be like to pedal great swaths of the country on a tandem bike. Along the way, we come to realize how unassuming and friendly they really are, which helps resolve one of the great mysteries of the book: how they manage to stay married through it all."
-Steve Horrell, retired reporter for the *Edwardsville (IL) Intelligencer*

"*Bicycling Historic Route 66* is more than just a travelogue; it's a journey of discovery that educates and entertains in equal measure. Tracy and Peter Flucke's adventure along the iconic Route 66 is filled with rich historical context, fascinating insights, and humorous anecdotes that make learning a joy. A must-read for adventurers, history buffs, and lifelong learners alike."
-Nick Burgraff, PhD, cycling enthusiast and physiologist

"Peter and Tracy always delight with their joyous posts about their tandem adventures. I love the "he says – she says" format as each perspective offers insight into what unfolds as they journey across iconic Route 66."
-Diane Jenks, host and producer of *The Outspoken Cyclist* **podcast**

"A fast and enjoyable read, Tracy and Peter's mile-by-mile concerns of weather, water, food, safety, and maintenance remind us of early motorists' priorities on the young and rugged US Highway 66."
-Cheryl Eichar Jett, author of *Route 66 in Illinois*

"I have yet to encounter anyone in my personal or professional experience who can surpass Tracy and Peter Flucke when it comes to bike safety expertise and endurance riding preparation."
-Attorney Jon R. Pinkert

"The clever way Tracy and Peter write their vivid daily logs makes you feel like you're on an extra seat of their tandem bike, yet needing to expend none of your own energy. They will even share a cold pint with you at brewery stops along the way."
-Cameron Teske, author of *Green Bay Beer: A History of the Craft*

More of What Others Are Saying

"Peter and Tracy's book brings to life many of the surprises, discomforts, and reasons you should go beyond your comfort zone. Riding a tandem together for 2,600 miles teaches us much about building endurance, companionship, relationships, and enthusiasm for life."
-Dan Burden, *National Geographic's* first bicycle touring photographer and author (May, 1973)

"Tracy and Peter Flucke illustrate what is wonderful about the bicycling community. The fulfilling interactions between travelers and hosts can be just as much a part of the journey as the ride itself."
-Tahverlee Anglen, Executive Director, Warmshowers.org Foundation

"Tracy and Peter Flucke deliver great insight into the joys and pains of long-distance biking, the obstacles you might have to overcome, and how you have to be ready for anything."
-Jacob VanSickle, Executive Director-Bike Cleveland and League of American Bicyclists-League Certified Cycling Instructor

"What sets this book apart is Tracy and Peter's love for exploration and local experiences. Their passion for cycling is matched only by their enthusiasm for visiting local breweries along the way. From savoring unique craft brews to discovering the heart and soul of the towns they pass, their love of the journey shines through."
-Andrew Fabry, Founder of Badger State Brewing Co.

"This book is not just about a bike trip. It also serves as a window into Tracy and Peter's relation-ship; a metaphor, if you will, for the life journey of a couple."
-Mark Owings, TandemDiversity.com

"We had many people stop by the café who were traveling Route 66 on their bicycle, but we never had anyone tandem-ride it. That's what fascinated me so much about Tracy and Peter. They were so sweet and complement each other."
-Fran Houser, former owner of the Midpoint Café in Adrian, Texas

Bicycling Historic Route 66

Our Adventure Crossing the USA
on a Bicycle Built for Two

Tracy & Peter Flucke

M&B Global Solutions Inc.
Green Bay, Wisconsin (USA)

Bicycling Historic Route 66

Our Adventure Crossing the USA on a Bicycle Built for Two

Front cover image: Tracy and Peter Flucke pose in front of the sign in Chicago, Illinois, marking the beginning of historic Route 66.

Back cover image: Tracy and Peter Flucke at the "End of the Trail" Route 66 sign on Santa Monica Pier in California.

ISBN: 978-1-942731-47-4

Printed by Seaway Printing Company Inc.
Green Bay, Wisconsin (USA)

Designed and published by M&B Global Solutions Inc.
Green Bay, Wisconsin (USA)

Dedication

To our parents,

Dorothy and Gil Meisner,

Ruth (Wiechmann) Flucke and Paul Flucke.

Thank you for instilling in us a sense of adventure,

and encouraging us to spread our wings ... and ride.

We love you forever and always.

Contents

We have seen the better part of the United States while riding our tandem, "Violet."

Preface

Peter

Tracy and I never intended to bicycle across the United States three times. Like much of life, it just kind of happened.

Tracy was born and raised in Wisconsin and her roots run deep. I, on the other hand, am a relative newcomer. Born in southern Minnesota, my parents were both Californians, so I guess that makes me first generation Midwest. We moved to Shorewood (a Milwaukee suburb), Wisconsin, when I was in middle school after spending five years in Syracuse, New York, and a year and a half in Honduras and Argentina. My father was a United Church of Christ minister for thirty-two years.

Both of us grew up camping and loving the outdoors. Tracy's family has rented a site on Campers Island in Lake Sinissippi near Hustisford in southeastern Wisconsin since the early 1960s.

The sixty-acre island was a forty-five-minute drive northwest from her childhood home in Wauwatosa (another Milwaukee suburb) and a fifteen-minute boat ride across the lake. The island has no electricity or running water. The lake and island sit just south of the Horicon National Wildlife

Refuge and the Horicon Marsh State Wildlife Area. Tracy spent most of her summers through elementary school on the island along with her two older brothers, younger sister, and mom. Her dad would join them on the weekends, driving up after work on Friday. Tracy considers the island paradise, and her ashes will be spread there someday.

Camping is what my family did during the summers when I was a kid living in Minnesota and New York. Dad took most of his vacation then because, as he jokingly used to say, "Nobody goes to church during the summer anyway." We had probably car camped/tented in half of the states by the time I was eleven years old. My younger brother and I originally shared a tent with our parents, but eventually graduated to a canvas army-surplus pup tent. It was small, hot, and leaked. There is an old family picture of me somewhere with a National Park Service Park Ranger and I am wearing his hat.

Neither of our families had any extra money in those days, so camping made a lot of sense. To us, it was normal.

Tracy was the jock in her family. She played center for the first ninth-grade girls basketball team at Hawthorn Junior High School. She played basketball, volleyball, and participated in track and field at Wauwatosa West High School. (Thank you, Title IX.) After high school, Tracy went to the University of Wisconsin-La Crosse, where she graduated with a degree in Recreation Administration. She was the first person in her family to attend college. Tracy played intramural sports during college and could dunk a volleyball in a regulation basketball hoop (I have witnesses). She is the true athlete of the two of us. I have never even touched the rim of a regulation basketball hoop.

I attended Shorewood High School, where I sang in the choir and musicals, played football (poorly), wrestled (okay), and competed in track and field (better). Fortunately, Shorewood is a small school, so everyone got to play. I enjoyed rock climbing at Devil's Lake State Park and backpacking throughout the country during the summers. I hiked 150 miles of the Appa-

It's not a stretch to say bikes have always been a big part of our lives.

lachian Trail in North Carolina and Tennessee with two buddies the summer after my sophomore year. The three of us hiked 200 miles of the John Muir Trail in the Sierra Nevada Mountains of California the following year. Academics were really Shorewood's thing, and luckily for me, I got caught in the college-bound wave and just barely made it in.

The first time I met Tracy was in the fall of 1984. I walked into the Iowa County (Wisconsin) Courthouse on unsteady legs, prepared to testify for the first time in a court case as a Blackhawk Lake Recreation Area summer park ranger. The charges were OWI (operating while intoxicated) and resisting arrest against a drunk motorcyclist. I was twenty-three years old and scared to death. I had made the two-and-a-half-hour drive from the University of Wisconsin-Stevens Point for the trial in a friend's car with a bulging tire. I was in the last semester of my senior year and would soon graduate with a degree in Recreation/Forestry and minors in Integrated Resource Management and Environmental Law Enforcement. I was going to be a park ranger. When I stepped into the assigned courtroom, I spotted my supervisor, Tom Presney, sitting in uniform in the fifth row with two of my fellow park rangers and a pretty young woman with long blond hair I did not know. I slid into the row next to the young woman and introduced myself, "Hi, I'm Peter Flucke."

"I'm Tracy Meisner, the assistant manager at Blackhawk," she said with a smile.

The biker entered a guilty plea before the trial and I did not have to testify.

Tracy and I reconnected in the spring of 1985. We were both working for American Adventure Inc., in the tourism hub of Wisconsin Dells. American Adventure was a nationwide membership campground company. She was a recreation programmer and I was a manager in training. Technically, I was her boss, and I wasn't very good at it. We both left the company after less than a year, but I eventually followed her to Hutchinson, Minnesota, where she was a recreation programmer and I started work at the police department. I progressed from parking enforcement officer to community service officer, and eventually became a part-time police officer. I liked law enforcement and seemed to have an aptitude for it, so I went to night school and eventually became a full-time, licensed Minnesota police officer.

Tracy and I were married at her family church in Wauwatosa in May of 1987.

In 1988, we moved to the Minneapolis/St. Paul area for new jobs. Tracy was a program director for the Minnesota Sports Federation (MSF) and I was a park ranger for the Suburban Hennepin Regional Park District (now the Three Rivers Park District). Tracy stayed with MSF for about a year and then moved on to the city of Savage, where she became their first parks and recreation director.

I was a full-time, licensed law enforcement officer and emergency medical technician (EMT) at Hennepin Parks. I had a badge, gun, Kevlar, the whole bit, but my title was park ranger and I got to wear a Stetson hat. I patrolled the district's 27,000 acres of parkland, north, west, and south of the metro by car, ATV, and foot, protecting both people and property. Two years into the job, I pitched the idea of using bicycles as patrol vehicles to park administration. The Seattle Police Department had recently started using bicycles and they seemed perfect for the parks. It was not easy, but I was eventually given permission to start one of the first police bicycle patrols in the state. I attended training from the International Police Mountain Bike Association (IPMBA) and added bicycle patrol officer to my title.

As a bicycle-trained police officer, I started to work with Cynthia McArthur, the director of Pedal Power Camp at the Minnesota Bike Safety Project. It was here I began to understand the three main components of bicycle safety: engineering, education, and enforcement.

Our first daughter, Melissa Marie Flucke, was born in November of 1990.

We participated in our first organized multi-day bicycle tour in the summer of 1991, when Melissa was less than a year old. The ride was a supported three-day fundraiser for the American Lung Association and followed the banks of the Mississippi River south from Minneapolis. The skies opened up with rain, thunder, and lightning as we arrived the morning of the ride. I am afraid of lightning, at least out in the open, but I really wanted to give this a try if Tracy did.

"You still want to do this?" I asked her.

"I'm in," she replied, and that was that.

We loaded our camping gear into the support truck and got our bicycles ready to go. Tracy was riding a Trek 820 hybrid with flat handlebars while I was riding a Trek 560 road bike with ram-style handlebars and skinny tires, and pulling six-month-old Melissa in a Burley D'lite trailer. I had purchased my Trek in college after trying to do my first triathlon on an ancient, and much heavier, Schwinn ten-speed. I can only imagine what the ride organizers were thinking when they saw us roll up. Within minutes, Tracy and I were completely soaked from the rain, but thank goodness, Melissa was warm and dry in her trailer with a rain cover. We warmed baby bottles in gas station microwave ovens, changed cloth diapers along the side of the road, camped in city parks, and had a wonderful time. We were hooked, although I did discover that I definitely needed a touring bike with lower gears to pull Melissa and her trailer up the steep river bluffs. We participated in the ride for the next three years, with me providing sag support for several days the last year while Tracy and Melissa rode with a friend.

I had burned out on law enforcement by early 1993. Too much stress and not enough sleep were doing me in and taking me away from my young family. I needed to get out. Tracy agreed to find a new job and was hired as the director of parks, recreation, and forestry for the village of Ashwaubenon (a Green Bay suburb), Wisconsin, in the spring. While Tracy was learning her new job, my job was to get us settled, take care of Melissa, and figure out what to do with the rest of my life. Easy! Every day, Melissa, now three years old, and I would explore greater Green Bay, especially the ball pit at the Hardee's restaurant near our rented house. We would go for a family bicycle ride in the country to the west of town every night after Tracy got home from work. The roads were flat, in good shape, and best of all, had very little traffic.

About this time, I figured out what I wanted to do with my life. I was appalled at how little most bicyclists and law enforcement officers knew about bicycle safety. As a trained recreation professional, law enforcement officer, and bike cop, the problem was obvious to me. I reasoned that if no one was training the bicyclists or the cops, how were things ever going to get better? I was going to become a bicycle safety consultant. I had never heard of one before, but that is what I was going to do.

Then it happened. In early May 1993, I got a telephone call from Joanne Pruitt Thunder from the Wisconsin Department of Transportation's Bureau of Transportation Safety. Joanne had heard from a colleague in Minnesota that I was starting my own bicycle safety consulting business and she wanted to know more about my plans. I told Joanne I wanted to develop a two-day course for law enforcement officers about bicycle safety.

"No one ever trains the cops." I said.

"How much will it cost?" she asked.

"Ten thousand dollars," I said with confidence off the top of my head.

"When can you start?" was her reply.

Nuts! I should have asked for more money. First lesson of business learned.

I taught my first "Enforcement for Bicycle Safety" course for Wisconsin law enforcement officers later that year. Since then, I have added pedestrian safety to the course and have taught it across the country. Our small, family-based company, WE BIKE, etc., LLC specializes in the areas of engineering, education, enforcement, and encouragement for walking, bicycling, and healthy communities.

Our second daughter, Alexandra Laurel Flucke, was born in March of 1995, and I became a nationally certified League Cycling Instructor with the League of American Bicyclist in 1996.

That same year, we bought our first tandem bicycle, a green Trek T-100 with flat handlebars and grip shifting ($1,500). We loved bicycling as a family, but with Melissa on her own two-wheeler by now and Alex in the trailer, we could not ride more than a couple of miles before Melissa had enough. We decided to outfit the back of the tandem with special pedals for Melissa, a kiddie crank, so we could ride farther. These pedals were high enough for Melissa to reach when she was perched behind me on the rear seat. Together, Melissa and I could ride like we did when she was in the bicycle trailer. The tandem was the answer to our problem. We continued our shorter family rides during the week, but on the weekends, we started to push our mileage. Eventually, we were able to ride to the NEW Zoo and back, thirty-five miles, and complete the Menominee River (metric) Century, sixty-two miles.

Tracy started work on her master's degree in public administration in 1995. She had a full-time job, two young children, and me to take care of. She graduated from the University of Wisconsin-Green Bay in 2000 and went on to become the first administrator for the town of Harrison, Wisconsin, in 2005 and then the administrator for the village of Allouez (another Green Bay suburb) in 2010.

In the late 1990s, Tracy decided she wanted to try and bicycle her first hundred-miler at the Door County Century. She was concerned that she would not be able to complete the ride on her own bike, so she asked me if we could do it together on the tandem. Sure! I had done the ride on my single road bike several times, so I thought it would be fun to do it on the tandem together. We started training several months before the event and completed it without a problem. During our training, we discovered we liked riding together on the same bike. The coordination and trust required to ride the tandem brought us closer, and boy could we make that bike move, at least on the flats and the downhills. The tandem, all tandems in fact, goes uphill like a brick.

We continued to ride the T-100 together, and by 2001 we were ready for a real road touring tandem. After painstaking research on my part, we decided on a 2000 Santana Arrive ($6,000). This was a serious investment for us. We had two colors to choose from, black or purple. Tracy chose purple and named the bike, "Violet." I had a blast outfitting the tandem for loaded touring and found that my backpacking skills came in very handy. Both sports require equipment that is lightweight, but durable.

Our first fully loaded trip on Violet was from our home in Ashwaubenon to my brother's hobby farm in Fond du Lac, sixty-five miles to the south. The trip along the east shore of Lake Winnebago was beautiful and we arrived with no problems. We set up our new tent by the pond on the back side of the property, made dinner, and went to bed. The next morning we made breakfast, packed up, and rode back home. It would have been a perfect trip had it not been for the ravenous mosquitoes. We were hooked. We never did see my brother. Ha-ha.

We continued to tour on Violet over the next thirteen years, mostly in the Midwest, taking longer and longer trips as time permitted. At this point in our lives, we were consumed with raising the girls and work, but somehow we knew that riding the tandem together was good for us as a couple. The family that rides together, stays together.

We were constantly looking for new and more challenging rides as our skills improved. Honestly, riding the same old bicycle trails and routes was getting boring. Beer to the rescue.

Tracy gave me the book *Wisconsin's Best Beer Guide*, by Kevin Revolinski, for Christmas in 2011 whereupon I announced, "Let's bike to them all."

"Okay," Tracy said.

We are not big drinkers, but we do like a good beer now and then. Planning our routes to the breweries gave us an excuse to further hone our navigation skills, and successfully bagging a new brewery and getting a pint glass boosted our confidence. (Note: This was prior to the explosion of microbreweries throughout the country and Wisconsin. We are woefully behind on our brewery quest these days.)

Cycling has always been a family affair for the Fluckes. Here we are in the late 1990s with our daughters Alexandra (Alex) on the left and Melissa, right.

I rolled over in bed one night and said to Tracy, "I think we should bicycle across the country. I don't want to wake up someday when it's too late and wish we had done it."

She looked at me, smiled, and said, "Okay!" (How did I get so lucky?)

We continued to take two-day, three-day, one- and two-week trips, but this time with a purpose. We were preparing for the adventure of a lifetime. By the time we could do three-week unsupported trips, I figured we could make it across the country. All we had to do was string a bunch of three-week trips together. Simple! Now for the hard part: when to do the trip.

Our girls were pretty well-launched by the summer of 2014. Melissa was attending graduate school at UW-La Crosse after completing her undergrad degree at the University of Minnesota-Twin Cities (UMN), and Alex was settled at UMN and would be spending the summer in Fiji learning to scuba dive, with sharks! My work tends to be a bit slower during the summer because most folks in my business are out riding their bikes. Tracy's job was the real problem.

Tracy had been working since she was in high school, including twenty-eight years in municipal government, and she was the primary breadwinner in our family. I never would have been able to start WE BIKE and be

There has never been agreement in our family about which of our daughters, Alex or Melissa, is with Peter here along the Fox River in Green Bay, Wisconsin. We just know it's a cool photo.

home with our girls without her income, insurance, and support.

There was a tremendous amount of change occurring politically in Wisconsin at the time, and this was adding to her already stressful job. Tracy would often go in to work at 7 a.m. and not get home until 11 p.m. She had achieved most of her work goals, so maybe it was time for a change. I think it was her bicycle commuting, twelve miles round trip, that kept her going as long as she did. Bottom line, Tracy was burned out!

Tracy is one of the hardest workers and most determined people I have ever met. While this is incredibly helpful on the tandem, it was eventually her undoing at work. The more difficult things got, the harder she worked. To keep her from imploding, we started to train for a cross-country bicycle trip. Just in case.

By this time, WE BIKE was doing well enough that I thought it could support our family. I would often tell Tracy on her bad days that she did not have to go back to work. If she would quit and come to work with me full-time, we could make a go of it. I was happy to support her as she had me when I left law enforcement some twenty-one years earlier. We would be alright, but in her struggles, she could not hear me. Eventually, I had to stage an intervention.

We went to our annual meeting with our financial advisor, Dan Balch from Woodmen Financial Resources, early in the year. I asked Dan if we could afford to have Tracy quit her job so we could bicycle across the country.

"Are we crazy? I asked Dan.

"What would be crazy is not to do it and then wish someday that you had," he replied. "If you don't change your current lifestyle much, you will be fine."

"I don't have to go back to work?" Tracy asked.

"No, I've been telling you that," I said.

It was decided!

During the summer of 2014 we successfully bicycled 4,362 miles unsupported on Violet across the Northern Tier of the United States from Bellingham, Washington, to Bar Harbor, Maine. The trip took us seventy-two days and was one of the hardest things we have ever done. It tested our marriage more than we had ever planned (see our book *Coast to Coast on a Tandem: Our Adventure Crossing the USA on a Bicycle Built for Two*), but we loved it!

Having crossed the country from west to east, I now wanted to cross it from north to south, and Tracy was game. The following year, we bicycled the length of the Mississippi River on the Mississippi River Trail (MRT). To accomplish this, we first bicycled from our home in Green Bay, north to International Falls, Minnesota, and the Canadian border. From there, we headed back south to Itasca State Park in northcentral Minnesota and the headwaters of the Mississippi River. From a mere stream to a mighty river, we followed the Mississippi to its southernmost point on the Gulf of Mexico, ninety miles south of New Orleans. In all, the trip lasted fifty days and covered 3,052 miles.

Now what?

***

Tracy and I never intended to write our first book, much less more than one. Like much of life, it just kind of happened. We "simply" wanted to see if we could ride across the country. We blogged and posted to Facebook daily during our trip to keep in touch with family and friends. There was never any thought of writing a book. (Although, both my father and grandfather were authors, so wouldn't it be cool if I was, too?)

It was not until several years after our Northern Tier journey that we even considered writing a book. Ultimately, it was the cries of "You should write a book," or "When are you going to write a book?" that got us moving in that direction. *Coast to Coast on a Tandem: Our Adventure Crossing the USA on a Bicycle Built for Two* was published in 2017.

The goals behind our first book were to entertain, educate, and inspire. After several years of sales, presentations, interviews, and reviews, I was finally confident we achieved our goals and could do it again through our second book. Maybe even better.

We wrote *Bicycling Historic Route 66* in a style similar to *Coast to Coast on a Tandem*. It is based on our blog and Facebook posts, and features both of our voices. Without both perspectives, you just wouldn't get the whole story.

"I felt like I was on the ride with you!" is the single best complement we received about our first book.

We hope you are similarly inspired, entertained, and educated this time as you accompany us on our bicycle trip along the length of historic Route 66.

Posing at Badger State Brewing Company in Green Bay with friends, family, and other supporters prior to embarking on our 2016 Route 66 bicycle adventure.

Introduction

Peter

It is the fall of 2015, the day is hot and humid, and getting long. We are battered and tired, and so is our tandem bicycle, "Violet." There has not been much to see for the past eighty-eight miles other than sawgrass and oil rigs, and there is a headwind. Pedaling the length of the Mississippi River on a bicycle built for two with one's spouse is not for the faint of heart. Fortunately, there is not much traffic and we are almost done.

We turn right on Jump Basin Road, which then curves right and becomes Tide Water Road. Three more miles and there it is, the sign:

Welcome
You Have Reached the Southernmost Point in Louisiana
Gateway to the Gulf

I reach my hand back to Tracy, and she grabs it and gives it a squeeze.

"Where do you want to go next?" she asks. "I have been thinking about that," I say.

"Surprise!" Tracy laughs.

"Well, we have now ridden west to east and north to south across the country. How about we get a little history and ride Route 66?" I suggest.

"Sounds good to me," Tracy replies.

And that is that!

The spring of 2016 was crazy busy for me. I guess you could say I was approaching the top of my game as a national pedestrian and bicycle safety consultant. Thank goodness Tracy was now working with me at our small, family-based consulting business, WE BIKE, etc., LLC. Spring is always a busy time for us, but this was exceptional. I felt like I was always on the road and barely had time to think, let alone plan for an unsupported cross-country bicycle trip.

The year started with an update of the two-day Pedestrian and Bicycle Law Enforcement Training Course I had developed for the Wisconsin Department of Transportation way back in 1993, and just kept going. In mid-March, we started doing a weekly *Better Biking* segment on the NBC26 Wisconsin Tonight show here in Green Bay with hosts Cassandra Duvall and John Maino, and then I headed to Idaho for its state safety summit and to teach a course for law enforcement officers. I followed that with two courses in New York State. I presented at the National Safe Routes to School conference in Columbus, Ohio, did another law enforcement course in Cleveland, Ohio, one in Wisconsin, and two more in New York in April. I was in Wisconsin for all of May, but I taught a course for Department of Natural Resources law enforcement rangers, and we did several Safe Routes to School presentations in the Fox Valley. I was exhausted!

Tracy

With all our work projects, and Peter traveling for many of them, I was handling everything at our home office, wrapping up projects with some clients, and notifying others about our planned break in services. Luckily, the slow time in our business is summer when "everyone" is out bicycling.

Simultaneously, I was trying to get organized for our upcoming bicycle trip. Preparing to be gone for up to two months is a project in itself. I needed to figure out who will take care of our cats, check on our house, how to pay bills, the technology needed for the trip, communicate with sponsors, etc. Although, it is easier this time because we have done it before.

Peter

We had learned a lot about training while preparing for our past two cross-country trips. Typically, we start training five to six months prior to a major ride, working on our flexibility, strength, and endurance, and so it was with this trip. Our six-day-a-week workouts alternated between strength and endurance training. They built up over time to six-hour training sessions (brick workouts) consisting of running, bicycling, and then more running at least once a week. This regime allowed us to endure up to eight hours a day on the bicycle under all types of conditions. We were ripped!

Tracy

Peter lost too much weight, and consequently some strength, on our first two trips. This, in my opinion, led to more grumpiness than normal. We do not want to go through that again! We felt there was room for improvement, specifically in strength maintenance and nutrition.

While our nutrition was already good, we needed to improve it for the rigors of the upcoming trip. Enter Lee Hyrkas, Registered Dietitian. Lee taught us how to improve and time our nutrition for maximum effect, along with how to avoid common pitfalls like food fatigue. (A human being can only eat so many Clif bars.)

Lee estimated that Peter burns 5,000-7,000 calories a day, and it is very difficult to eat enough food to get that many calories. He taught us how to supercharge what we eat; for example, by adding peanut butter, nuts, dried fruit, etc., to our instant oatmeal in the morning. Lee also explained when to eat certain foods to get the most benefit; for example, eating high-protein foods (milk, string cheese, yogurt, etc.) within an hour of completing our daily rides. This allows our bodies to start rebuilding muscle as soon as possible for the next day's effort. We always carry a small jar of peanut butter and tortillas on the bike now, just in case.

With our nutrition well in hand, Peter still felt he needed to do something to maintain more strength and flexibility during the trip. Our trainer, Nate Vandervest, CSCS, CES, created four ten-minute, body-weight workouts that Peter could do anywhere on a rotating basis. (See chart on next page.) The idea was to keep the muscles firing to hopefully slow, if not prevent, atrophy. He was able to maintain this routine until about halfway through the trip, then it was every muscle for itself.

Peter

I took the tandem to JB Cycle & Sport in Howard (a suburb of Green Bay) in early February for a tune-up. The "boys" had been taking care of "Violet" since we bought her back in 2001. There was really nothing wrong with the bike, but she was sixteen years old and had over 50,000 miles on her, many of those being tough, loaded touring miles. It seemed like a good idea to get her checked by a professional before the trip. Their only recommendation was to replace the wheel rims, which were original. When I asked if there was anything wrong with them, they told me, "No, but they are kind of old."

"Well, if there is nothing wrong with them, I think they will be fine," I said.

Tracy

We are frequently asked how we find our way across the country. "Is there a trail?" No, the majority of the time we are sharing public roads with motorists. Fortunately, Adventure Cycling Association (ACA) has maps designed specifically for bicycle tourists that highlight mostly low-volume roads and

Peter's strength training routine

Upper body strength

YTWL	:30 holds
Reverse flys	2 x 10
Push-ups	2 x 10-15
Picnic table recline pull-ups	2 x 8
Inchworms	2 x 8

Flexibility

Kneeling hip flexor	:30 each
Kneeling quad	:30 each
Reach and rotate	8 each side
Press ups	10
Calf stretch	:30 each
Side bend	:30 each
Left over right visa verse	:30 each

Lower body activation

Lateral lunge	8 each
Forward lunge	8 each
Backward lunge	8 each
Double leg calf raise	20
Single leg calf raise	15 each
Hip hikes	15 each
Line hops lateral	:30

Core strength

Front plank	:30
Side plank	:30
Glute bridge	:30
Single leg glute bridge	:30 each
Scapular push-ups	15 reps
Bird dogs	10 reps each
Active straight leg raises	10 reps each

the services we need like water, food, lodging, and bicycle shops. On this trip, we will also be using Bob Robinson's *Bicycling Guide to Route 66*. Peter's phone with Google Maps can be helpful for navigating, but frequently there is no connectivity. (MapMyRide, Ride with GPS, etc., were not available or popular at the time.) The GPS tracker we will be carrying will allow friends and family to follow our progress 24/7. This will not help us to navigate, but it will enable others to find us!

Our cats supervised Tracy as she prepared essentials that we would carry through-out our trip.

On the bike, food is fuel, and we cannot afford to run out. We typically carry breakfast supplies, two freeze-dried dinners, and lots of miscellaneous snacks. We try to eat two meals a day at restaurants, but cannot guarantee they will be available. The food we carry on the bike just barely gives us enough calories to survive. Regardless, we need to supplement our on-bike food regularly. Think gas station/convenience stores and grocery stores.

Peter

Our equipment is pretty well locked down by this point. We have learned what we need from all our previous trips. We carry approximately fifty-five pounds of gear, and with that we are able to make most repairs to the bike, camp, and cook our own meals. The only atypical pieces of equipment we are carrying on this trip are a small laptop computer and an MSR Dromedary Bag. The computer is for blogging and watching movies, and the water bag is to supplement our six 24-ounce water bottles due to the extreme conditions we are expecting.

Adventure Cycling Association (ACA)

"A nonprofit organization, Adventure Cycling Association's mission is to inspire, empower, and connect people to travel by bicycle. Established in 1993 as Bikecentennial, they are the premier bicycle-travel organization in North America with more than 54,000 members."

https://www.adventurecycling.org/

Safety is always a consideration on the bike, although our risk is relativity low. According to the National Highway Traffic Safety Administration, in 2016, 37,461 people died in motor vehicle crashes, including 840 bicyclists (2.24 percent). Things we do to improve our safety include wearing helmets, traveling on low-volume roads whenever possible, wearing bright-colored clothing, displaying a slow-moving vehicle sign, always using front and rear lights, and not riding at night. The tracker we carry also provides a degree of safety.

Additionally, we are well-trained cyclists and instructors. We know what the leading causes of bicyclist crashes are and how to avoid them.

As for our personal safety, we have never, even once, in all our years of bicycle touring had an issue. Although, if an issue does come up, we have an advantage in that I have training as a police officer, black belt in karate, and pressure point control tactics instructor.

Tracy

We also have a code word that Peter can use if he feels he needs to fight and I should go for help.

While we are confident we have done everything within our control to prepare for this trip, we are careful not to fall into the trap of overconfidence. There is a saying in the bicycling community, "On a bicycle, you don't have to look for adventure, adventure will find you." Our professional training and previous long-distance bicycling experiences make us well aware of this.

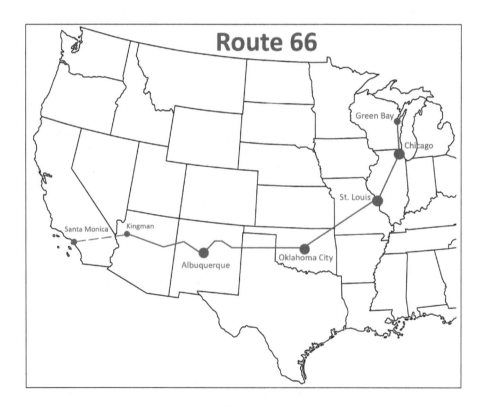

The beginning of our journey featured a posed photo with our tandem, "Violet," in front of a 1925-vintage Polo-Resto Service Station in De Pere, Wisconsin.

Chapter 1

State of Wisconsin

June 3-6, 2016
263 miles/263 total

Day 1
June 3 - Green Bay to Mishicot, Wisconsin
42 miles (total miles – 42)
Sunny, 70 degrees with a light headwind

Peter

We are done with breakfast and dressed in our bicycling clothes: bright, high-tech jerseys, padded shorts, socks, and shoes. The dishes are washed, beds are made, garbage emptied, window shades adjusted, night-light timer set, and we have done the final walkthrough of the house, twice. It is strange not having our two cats underfoot. It is time to bicycle historic Route 66. We are so excited!

"Are you ready to go?" I ask Tracy.

"I think so," she says.

I slide the GPS tracker into the middle of my three back jersey pockets and push the lighted button on the garage wall to open the big metal door to the outside. It slowly rises to reveal a beautiful, cool, sunshiny day.

Our purple tandem bicycle, "Violet," companion of so many miles, is leaning against the back end of our aging Toyota minivan, loaded and ready to go.

We step into the garage, and while I slide between our two commuter bikes and the also-aging Toyota Prius to get my bicycle helmet and gloves from the shelf by the garage door, Tracy double-locks the house door behind us.

I grasp the tandem by the handlebars, pull it gently away from the back of the van and into a balanced position on its two narrow tires. Carefully, I turn the handlebars and begin to walk the bike out of the garage onto the driveway and point it slightly downhill toward the street. The bike is much more difficult for me to maneuver when it is loaded like this with the four panniers (bicycle bags), tent, and six large water bottles. We carry fifty-five pounds of gear, not counting the water. Violet is much like a penguin out of water until both of us are on board and we are pedaling smoothly.

Tracy puts on her helmet and gloves, and is standing by the outside garage door keypad, ready to close and lock the door.

"Got everything?" I ask.

"I sure hope so," she says, and closes the garage door. This is the last time we will close this door for two months.

I step my leg over the bike's top tube while squeezing the brakes for stability, and straddle the bike with both feet planted firmly on the ground.

Tracy says, "You ready for me?"

"I'm ready," I say.

Tracy grasps the bike's rear handlebars, climbs onto the back seat, and clips her cycling shoes with downhill ski-like bindings into the pedals. I hear a "click, click."

"Ready," she says.

I clip my right foot into the pedal, move it into the up ("power pedal") position, and say, "Ready, up." I step down on the clipped-in pedal as Tracy starts to add power, clip in my other foot, and we are moving. I know to

Facebook comments from our first day

"Good luck! Have fun!" - **Paula Roberts (cross-country tandem cyclist)**
"Enjoy your adventure, safe travels and may the wind always be at your back!" - **Judy Judd**
"Can't wait to follow your adventures! Have fun, be safe!" - **Heidi-Lynn Arvey**
"Good luck and safe travels" - **Linda Shimek**
"Have fun!" - **Susan Johnson**
"Good luck!! Hope you have a great time!!" - **Christine Healey**
"Best of Luck" - **Kathy Crain Wondrash**
"Good luck!" - **Mary Gorton (our backyard neighbor)**
"AWESOME!!! TRAVEL SAFE!" - **Katie Hafsoos Commer (Tracy's childhood best friend)**
"Good luck on your trip!" - **Bobbie Fredericks**
"Have fun and be safe!" - **Chad Carter (friend and athletic trainer)**
"Safe travels!!!" - **Joshua Ray**
"Have a safe trip!" - **Peggy Olson**
"Living vicariously through you two! Safe travels and post often!" - **Kathi Hegranes**
"Safe travels with many adventures and good times!" - **Cathy Skott (Warmshowers guest)**
"Good luck and safe travels!!!" - **Lisa Devroy**
"God's speed and safe travels, can't wait to get the updates!!!" - **Mary Jane Clements Quass**
"Have a wonderful and safe trip!!!" - **Kathy Lukes Faust**
"Good luck on this next adventure. Safe travels Fluckes." - **Allison Kay Nesbitt**

almost immediately call out, "Left turn," followed quickly by "Bump," as we thump through the road gutter at the end of our short driveway and turn left up the Hawthorn Road hill.

We have mounted this bike tens of thousands of times and are quite comfortable and efficient doing it. Having said that, we did mess up once in a friend's driveway with their entire family watching. We were all casually chatting, and Tracy thought she heard me say, "Ready." She jumped up on the bike, whereupon I lost control. Tracy unceremoniously crashed onto the bike's top tube and then onto the ground. She was in a lot of pain, but was too embarrassed to admit it. She popped up, we regrouped, remounted, and rode away. Starting the tandem is even trickier when fully loaded, at least at first.

We climb the short, one-block, hill from our house to the corner more slowly than normal because of the extra weight on the bicycle and the fact we are not warmed up yet. We pass Mary and Will's house on our left, Roger and Barb's on the right. We have known most of our neighbors for more than twenty years. At the top of the hill, we turn right, passing the water tower on our left. I quickly upshift several times by pushing the right shift/brake lever with my index and middle fingers as we slowly pick up speed. Two blocks down the road, we pass Frank and Susan's house on the right.

It is too early for their dog, Pa'lante, to be outside begging us to stop and play ball. (Pa'lante comes from a Spanish slang word loosely translated as "onward, "go ahead," or "go for it." It is not a word you will find in any standard Spanish dictionary. In fact, Spanish teachers might even cringe upon hearing it. Still, how appropriate for the start of our trip!)

We stop at the stop sign at Waube Lane. Our process is for me to say, "Stopping," as I gently squeeze both brakes, unclip one foot, and step to the ground. We balance the bike while Tracy stays clipped in and seated. Leaving Tracy on the bike simplifies and speeds up the process of stopping and restarting, unless we lose our balance.

We turn left on Waube Lane, right on South Ridge Road, then left on Parkview Road. We are now riding through the village of Ashwaubenon's industrial park with several hundred businesses. We pick up speed as we cruise down the Parkview hill at 15 mph. Soon, though, I have to break hard to slow down our roughly 450-pound total weight for the unmarked diagonal railroad tracks at the bottom of the hill.

To avoid catching our front wheel in one of the rail flanges and crashing, I (we) need to cross the tracks as close to perpendicular as possible. Since these particular tracks cross from my near right to my far left, I need to move us to the middle of the road from near the curb, and then angle sharply back to the right toward the curb. We do not take these particular railroad tracks, or any tracks for that matter, for granted. Several years ago, Tracy crashed on them while bicycling home from a meeting at night in the rain. Since it was a late meeting, I had gone to bed before Tracy got home. I did not realize until the next morning when I woke up and saw her scratched and bruised body next to me that she had crashed.

Tracking technology let people follow our progress

"Want to follow us live 24-7? Thanks to our sponsor, From the Finish Line, and its tracker technology - you can!" (Followers could click on a now-inactive link to track our progress.)

Our tracker, based on Global Positioning System (GPS) technology, was originally developed in Europe for child and extreme skiers, and multi-day endurance athletes. The tracker adds a level of safety by allowing friends and family to follow the carrier's progress live. The company reached out to us to pilot test the tracker for a multi-day, long-distance event, and we were happy to help. This technology is now commonly available in bicycle computers and smartwatches.

"What the hell happened to you?!" I asked.

She was otherwise uninjured, except for her pride.

There are two types of bicyclists, those who have fallen, and those who are about to fall. We do everything in our power to remain in the past-tense category.

I say to Tracy, "Check back." She looks over her left shoulder for traffic and says, "Clear," letting me know it is safe to move to the middle of the lane. We cross the tracks with ease and continue on our way. We are less than one mile from home.

We cross the intersection of Business Highway 41 and a perpendicular set of railroad tracks, and enter the city of De Pere. At the Brown County Fairgrounds, we turn right on Broadway and slide into the bicycle lane. Shortly, we cross another set of diagonal railroad tracks, but the bike lane is angled to help us cross these tracks at a right angle without interfering with traffic. We wind our way through the one-way streets in West De Pere until we reach St. Norbert College and the west end of the Claude Allouez Bridge over the Fox River.

The bridge gives us access to the Fox River State Recreational Trail along the east bank of the river below the bridge. The bridge is four lanes wide with bicycle lanes and separated oversized sidewalks. With a 25-mph speed limit, the bike lane is comfortable to ride, except for the occasional knucklehead driving 45 mph. "Really, dude!"

There is a two-lane roundabout at the east end of the bridge. I have the option of following the bike lane up onto the oversized sidewalk to a trail spur, which will wrap us around down and under the bridge to the main trail. The only problem with this option is a very tight turn between the sidewalk and the trail spur. Normally, we can make this turn if I am very careful, Tracy gently leans with me, and she doesn't panic. Tracy never thinks we will make the turn. Ha-ha! However, with the panniers and the extra weight on the bike, there is no way we can make the turn today. Instead, we go with option number two, which is to use the road and the roundabout.

"Check back," I call out to Tracy, and she calls back, "Clear."

I slide the bike into the middle of the right-turn lane and look left into the roundabout for approaching traffic in the near lane. Although roundabouts are intimidating to some bicyclists, as well as motorists, we know their slow speeds and lack of left turns make them the safest type of intersection. We are always glad when we encounter them, given the alternative, especially if we don't need to stop. Traffic is light this time, so we roll right into the roundabout and exit immediately onto South Broadway. Three blocks to the south, we turn right onto Bomier Street, and then take a quick left onto the Fox River Trail. We have traveled all of four miles.

The Fox River State Recreational Trail is near and dear to our hearts. When we moved to Ashwaubenon in the early 1990s, we thought we had died and gone to bicycling hell. There was not a single mile of recreation trail or bicycle lane in Northeastern Wisconsin. We had lived in the Twin Cities area of Minneapolis/St. Paul, Minnesota, where trails and bicycle lanes are commonplace. We just couldn't understand why there were not any bicycle facilities here.

Fortunately, around the time we moved, we met staff from the Wisconsin Department of Natural Resources (DNR) who were working on a plan to convert the state's hundreds of miles of abandoned railroad corridors into recreational trails. We also met, and joined, a local group of like-minded people known as the Friends of the Fox River Trail. The Friends' mission was to assist Brown County and the DNR in converting the abandoned Wisconsin Central LTD Railroad corridor along the eastern side of the Fox River from the city of Green Bay fourteen miles south to Greenleaf into a non-motorized recreational trail.

The Friends, Brown County, and DNR had lots of good intensions, but they also had some opposition. The northern six miles of the railroad corridor between Green Bay and De Pere ran through a residential area and often separated homes from the river. Some people who once accepted trains running through their back yards now claimed the quiet abandoned corridor as their own. One guy had actually covered the tracks with dirt and was growing vegetables on top of them. There was no way these people were going to let anyone run a trail through "their property."

A bitter fight ensued in which a small group of residents who lived along a particularly narrow section of the corridor challenged the federal rail banking legislation that allowed the abandoned railroad corridor to be held in the public trust and transferred to the DNR. Concerns included property rights, public safety, noise, garbage, and loss of produce. Several years of legal fighting resulted in the legislation being upheld, whereupon the DNR took control and leased the corridor to Brown County, which was charged with developing it into a state recreational trail.

The Fox River Trail opened in 2001, and since then more than three million people have used the trail. The Friends group continues to be deeply involved with protecting and improving the trail, including a $2.1 million

We did an interview with our local NBC affiliate before hitting the road.

capital fundraising campaign for drainage work, resurfacing, and addition of amenities. As of this writing, Tracy is the president of the Friends of the Fox River Trail.

Tracy

We head a short distance north on the Fox River Trail for a final press conference prior to leaving the Green Bay metro area. The historic Polo-Resto Service Station (1925), complete with vintage glass gas pumps and located adjacent to the trail in Voyager Park, is the perfect backdrop for the event. This is the first of many interesting old buildings we will likely see when we reach historic Route 66. A reporter from NBC26 in Green Bay is already there when we arrive, and we quickly get set for the interview. We know many of the reporters, assignment editors, and station managers in the Green Bay television market, and typically receive coverage about our bicycle adventures and are interviewed for bicycle- and pedestrian-related stories.

Our marketing specialist, Kathryn "Kat" Kroll, is handling our public relations/social media for the trip. Kat will be reaching out to media contacts

We ended our first day in Mishicot, Wisconsin, with a nice dinner and overnight visit with Tracy's Aunt Florence.

in communities we will travel through to set up interviews, creating a media bubble in front of us. We have never used this strategy before and are excited to see how much interest we receive. This is a great way to educate people about the importance of accommodating bicyclists, and others, in their community.

Linda O'Keefe, from GO Ride, a local woman's road riding group I belong to, is at the press conference. Linda plans to ride the first ten miles with us. It is great to have company at the start of our trip as we head south on the trail. When it is time for Linda to say goodbye, we get hugs and head off in opposite directions. It is bittersweet to say goodbye, knowing we will be on our own for the next couple of months and will miss our friends and family. But at the same time, we are excited about the adventures we will undoubtedly have.

Our route south eventually takes us off the Fox River Trail and onto quiet country roads as we head east to our first stop in the town of Maribel, where we enjoy lunch at a local restaurant. The last ten miles of the day to the village of Mishicot are beautiful as we travel through quiet Wisconsin farm country.

We will spend the night in Mishicot (pop. 1,402) at my Aunt Florence's house. Florence, who is eighty-six years old, is my mother's sister-in-law, and has graciously agreed to host us this evening. We take Florence out to dinner at one of her favorite restaurants, and then enjoy an evening of conversation and family. All too soon, it is time for bed. We know we need to get an early start in the morning.

Day 2
June 4 – Mishicot to Cedarburg, Wisconsin
87 miles (total miles – 129)
60 degrees, rainy with a headwind

Peter

We are up by 6:30 a.m., pack, have a light breakfast with Aunt Florence, and are on the road by 8 a.m. The temperature is in the low sixties, there is a south wind (headwind) at 5-12 mph, and a chance of rain in the afternoon. Wearing bicycle shorts and jerseys, we are comfortable once we get moving.

Our route starts on Highway 147 and takes us seven miles south to the city of Two Rivers on Lake Michigan, where we stop for a quick second breakfast at a fast-food restaurant. With years of bicycle touring experience and having worked with a sports nutritionist, we are acutely aware of our nutritional needs. I burn between 5,000 and 7,000 calories a day while touring, and I do not hold up well to the rigors of touring when I am not well-fed. We meet several customers at the restaurant who pepper us with questions about our trip.

"Where are you from?" "Where are you going to?"

Apparently, we and our fully loaded tandem don't look like we are from around here.

"Green Bay." "Santa Monica, California, via historic Route 66."

"On a bicycle?" "How far is that?"

We get the same questions over and over again, and we love it.

With breakfast number two rounding our bellies, we ride a few easy blocks east to the Mariner Trail, which is right on Lake Michigan. We follow the trail six more miles south to the city of Manitowoc. The trail is flat, smooth, and beautifully landscaped by local service clubs, but it is the unobstructed views of the lake to the east, our own inland sea, that capture our attention. So much blue. The only downside to the ride is the temperature. It is pretty cool along the lake – think mid-fifties and with that south breeze in our face. We are still fine with just our jerseys and shorts because we are working to move the loaded bicycle, but our light jackets are not far from our minds.

Tracy

I am very familiar with Two Rivers and Manitowoc. My mom grew up in Two Rivers and my dad in Manitowoc. I spent many happy weekends and holidays visiting my grandparents and exploring the area.

I believe my dad's dad is the one to blame for my love of moving under my own power. Grandpa Meisner had a little pedal surrey. It had four wheels and three bench seats, two under a beautiful red and white canopy, and another smaller one hanging off the front of the surrey. The front bench seat under the canopy had a steering wheel and pedals for two. All four of us grandkids (me, my sister, and two goofy brothers) could ride on the surrey at once. We would pedal all around the neighborhood and to the local ice cream/cheese shop. We spent many hours happily pedaling after our grandpa. Although, having two older brothers, I did have to fight to drive and pedal. Tears usually helped convince Grandpa to let me have a turn.

Once through Manitowoc, we follow Lake Shore Drive south twenty-six miles to the city of Sheboygan and a stop for lunch. It is a great road with little traffic and more amazing views of Lake Michigan. We will miss this.

> # Warmshowers.org Foundation explained
>
> "Warmshowers.org Foundation is a nonprofit hospitality exchange service for people engaging in bicycle touring. The website platform is a gift economy that provides the technology for reciprocal (free) hospitality for cyclists and hosts. What started as a personal spreadsheet of names more than a decade ago is now a community of more than 185,000 users across the globe."
> (https://www.warmshowers.org/)

Peter

After lunch, and with the skies threatening rain, we work our way south to the village of Oostburg and the Ozaukee Interurban Trail. Just as we get on the trail, the sky lets loose. We are completely soaked within minutes. Well, at least we can't get any wetter. Fortunately, the trail is paved and in good shape. It is easier, and probably safer right now, to ride the trail than the road given the rain. I really should put fenders on this bike someday.

Tracy

The village has created a great trailhead for the Ozaukee Interurban Trail, with restrooms and a kiosk featuring maps and other trail information. The trail continues thirty-six miles south to the city of Mequon. It is well-marked except when we enter one of the numerous communities located along it. The signage is often confusing or nonexistent, which makes it difficult, and sometimes impossible, to follow the trail. We get lost in Port Washington trying to find the trail again and must ride on a county road for about five miles. The road spray from the passing cars is not fun. Eventually, we find our way back to the trail, which is good because we are able to get away from the road spray and begin to dry out a bit.

We finally make it to the city of Cedarburg (pop. 11,515). We are staying here tonight with a couple through the Warmshowers.org Foundation program. (We'll refer to it simply as Warmshowers after this.) I logged into the Warmshowers website (https://www.Warmshowers.org Foundation/) before we left home to see if there were hosts available here. After checking several personal pages and reviews, I sent messages to a couple of them.

Two hosts responded that they could put us up for the night. Presumably, they checked our personal page and reviews, and figured we were okay. We decided to stay with Val and Bob, and thanked a host named Keith for his offer.

Peter

The sun finally comes out just as we arrive in Cedarburg. Val and Bob, our Warmshowers hosts, had told us about the local Silver Creek Brewery, which of course we must check out after our somewhat trying day. We were mostly dry, except for our shoes, by the time we arrived at the brewery. The brewery is housed in the former Cedarburg Mill, built in 1855 on the bank of Cedar Creek. It is nice to see this historic building being preserved and put to good use. Since we are filthy and cold, we have just one beer and purchase a commemorative glass before heading to our hosts' house, half a mile away.

Val and Bob live in a beautiful 1920s home. After a much-needed warm shower, we get acquainted and have a lovely dinner. Val and Bob got involved with Warmshowers because their daughter did a long bike tour recently and had used its service. They wanted to pay it forward. What great folks!

> ### Facebook comments from our stop at Silver Creek Brewery
>
> Made it to Cedarburg and the Silver Creek Brewery. - **Peter Flucke**
>
> **Pam Adams (Peter's high school friend)**
> Is this a bike trip or brewery tour? XO
>
> **Peter Flucke** - Um, yes?
>
> **Mandy Barringer (Northern Tier trip rescuer from our book *Coast to Coast on a Tandem*)**
> It always ends at a brewery here.
>
> **Peter Flucke**
> One of our favorite things about your family.

The day started out a bit tough, dealing with the rain and getting lost several times, but ended very nicely. This seems to happen often on our adventures and is usually the result of some act of kindness.

Tomorrow, we head to Racine and will be traveling the stretch from Cedarburg to Milwaukee with the other Warmshowers host from Cedarburg who responded to us. Keith reached out to us again earlier this evening to see if he and a buddy could ride with us to Milwaukee tomorrow. Of course! It will be nice to have the company.

We snuggle into bed early, with severe thunderstorms expected later this evening, wondering how many such storms this historic house has endured over nearly a century.

Day 3
June 5 – Cedarburg to Racine, Wisconsin
52 miles (total miles – 181)
Partly cloudy, 70 degrees, with a cross/tailwind

Tracy

After a nice visit and breakfast with Val, we head to the Cedarburg Community Gym to meet Keith and his friend, Rob. They will be bicycling to Milwaukee with us, and we are excited to head south on the Ozaukee Interurban Trail (OIT).

Peter

Keith and Rob are probably both in their mid-thirties and ride together a couple of times a week on the local trails, but this will be the first time they have gone all the way (twenty miles) to Milwaukee. Their wives and kids will drive down later to meet them for brunch and bring them home after a day in the big city.

When we reach the Milwaukee County line, just south of Mequon, the OIT becomes the Oak Leaf Trail, and we continue south.

Tracy

Peter lived in the village of Shorewood, on Lake Michigan just north of Milwaukee, when he was in middle and high school. He got really animated when we biked through Estabrook Park and over Capitol Drive on the old railroad bridge. Pointing, he said, "There used to be a Big Boy restaurant right there, and I would get a diet soda at that gas station on my way home after wrestling practice every day." We could see the Shorewood High School Copperdome and the athletic field where he ran track and played football to our left. Go Greyhounds! We were less than a mile from his old house on Larkin Street.

Keith and Rob do all the navigating, and we easily land in downtown Milwaukee by 9:30 a.m. A coffee shop near the Public Market in the Historic Third Ward provides us with a snack, coffee, and a chance to get to know each other better while we wait for their families to arrive.

The Historic Third Ward (HTW) is listed on the National Register of Historic Places as Milwaukee's oldest center of commerce and warehousing. Today the HTW is home to over 500 businesses and maintains an unparalleled position within the retail and professional service community as Milwaukee's showcase mixed-use district. The opening of the indoor Milwaukee Public Market in 2005 further enhanced the district.

When Keith and Rob's families arrive, the hugs, kisses, and energy are contagious. We join in the fun briefly, but then have to say goodbye to our new friends and continue on our way.

Once we are clear of Milwaukee, we stop for lunch in the city of South Milwaukee at Barberie's Italian restaurant. I worked as a waitress in high

We got to spend the night of our third day on the road with our good friends Doug and Kim Instenes in Racine, Wisconsin.

school for the Barberie's in Wauwatosa. The food was as good as I remember, and all the carbs will easily get us the next fifteen miles to the city of Racine (pop. 77,185).

Peter

We continue to Racine after lunch, where we are spending the night with our good friends Doug and Kim Instenes and their son, Daylen. Doug and I were best friends in middle school and high school, and we are still close today. I was the jock of the two of us, but we shared a love of music. Through countless hours in choir and musicals, we forged a lasting relationship, one that easily survived us taking the same girl to different school dances on double dates. Neither of us married that girl; we always came first. Doug was the best man in Tracy and my wedding, and I stood up in his wedding over thirty years ago. Doug is the managing/artistic director of the Racine Arts Guild.

We arrive in Racine by 3:30 p.m. and have plenty of time for a great visit, dinner, and dessert. All too soon though, it is time to get organized for the next day and hit the hay. We both are tired and ready for bed. There are severe thunderstorms tonight, but again, we are safe, warm, and dry with friends.

Navigating the trail system on the way to Chicago wasn't always as obvious as we would have liked. Here is Peter during a break on a gorgeous, cool day.

Day 4
June 6 – Racine, Wisconsin, to Chicago, Illinois
82 miles (total miles – 263)
Partly cloudy, 70 degrees with a slight tailwind

Tracy

Our visit with Doug and Kim was wonderful, but far too short. We take off early toward Chicago. Good thing, too, because we get lost just trying to find our way out of Racine. Oh no, is this going to be one of those days?

Peter

It is hard to leave Doug and Kim. Doug and I have been friends for more than forty years. We do not get time to see them often enough.

As luck would have it, the father of a friend from Green Bay (Chad Carter) lives in Racine, and Bob had asked what our route would be out of town. It is a pleasant surprise to see Bob waiting to meet us along the Root River Pathway on the south side of town. Normally, Bob would have ridden with us for a while, but today he has other commitments. We chat for a few minutes and then are on our way. Nice to meet you, Bob!

The route to our Warmshowers stay on the north side of Chicago is challenging. Surprisingly, the issue is not the traffic, rather the maze of trails we are trying to follow. The trails are in good condition generally, but they are full of twists, turns, and spurs which make navigation difficult, and we get lost several times. Also, there are frequent stops at cross streets, which severely slows our progress and tires us out. The tandem is a beast to stop and start frequently because of the weight and the balance required.

Tracy is the navigator on the bike. My logic has always been that since, as the captain/driver of the bike, I am primarily responsible for keeping us from crashing and must focus on the road in front of me. Tracy can look around and ride hands-free if needed. It is much safer to have her be the one reading any paper maps or using the digital map on my phone, and then telling me where to go.

Tracy

Sometimes I would really like to tell him "where to go."

Peter

Anyone who has ever tried to navigate on a road trip with their partner knows where this is heading.

I started learning to navigate on family camping vacations before I was old enough to read. My mother would have me read the roadmap with her to keep me occupied. Thanks, Mom! As I became older, I developed a keen interest in the great outdoors and backpacking, where navigation skills are essential. I studied recreation and forestry in college and there, if you couldn't navigate on your own, you would fail class and probably miss the field trip bus home for dinner. As a police officer, park ranger, and bike cop in Minnesota in my late twenties and early thirties, knowing where I was at all times was critical to my safety and those I was sworn to protect. I enjoy the challenge of navigating. Tracy, not so much.

The problems with my tandem-navigational logic are many. First, Tracy doesn't enjoy navigating as much as I do. Who does? Second, I have been known to yell at her when she makes a mistake. Completely unfair, I know. Experience and better nutrition have made me a more empathetic captain. Sorry, Honey! Third, riding on the back of the bicycle, Tracy cannot see directly in front of us. My helmeted head blocks roughly thirty degrees of her view. She can't see what I can see, and I cannot read her map. Finally, not all maps are created equally (sometimes north is at the top and sometimes not), and sometimes online maps are not detailed enough, inaccurate, slow to load, or simply will not load.

From the front of the bike, I am often concerned that we are off course. Unnecessary detours cost us precious physical and emotional energy, and time.

As we struggle to negotiate this sticky honeycomb of trails, I am constantly asking Tracy, "Do I turn here?" "Here?" The tandem handles much more like a semi-tractor tailor than a sedan, and I need extra time and space to maneuver. We are traveling much more slowly than normal and must stop frequently to use our combined resources to plan our next move.-

Because of our exceedingly slow pace, we call our Warm Showers host, twice, to tell them we will be arriving at their house later than expected. Our first estimated time of arrival was 5 p.m. and our second was 6:30 p.m.

Tracy

Luckily, late in the day when almost all hope is lost (and us, too), we meet a gentleman who is heading home from a bicycle ride on the trails. Christopher graciously leads us through the complex trail network, bringing us to Devon Avenue in the Edgewater Neighborhood, our trail jumping-off point. It is so nice to follow someone who knows where he is going. Christopher is an interesting man and gives us lots of history about the trail system. From where Christopher leaves us, we have about fifteen miles left to get to our Warmshowers stay just north of downtown Chicago.

Peter

In Edgewater, we have to navigate about four miles of heavy urban rush-hour traffic east to Lake Michigan, but it is a nice change from the trails. Once we reach the lake, we head south on the Lake Front Trail for another five miles of easy navigating to our Warmshowers stay. Wow, there are a lot of people on this trail. Fun!

We finally arrive at our hosts' home at 7:30 p.m., two and a half hours later than expected. It has been a long day. Fortunately, Rod and Laura are very understanding. Over a dinner of Chinese takeout, we get to know our hosts, who are parents of two teenagers, and begin to understand why they are so chill. Amazingly, they spent two years biking around the world in their twenties. You should hear their stories! Also, Rod worked for the bicycle manufacturer Cannondale in his younger years, and now owns his own business. Cool people.

After much conversation, it is time to get ready for the next day and invest in some much-needed sleep.

Tomorrow, we ride to downtown Chicago and the official start of historic Route 66!

This photo opportunity with Buckingham Fountain and the Chicago skyline was a nice welcome to our day in the city.

Chapter 2

State of Illinois

June 7-14, 2016
379 miles/642 total

Day 5
June 7 - Chicago to Joliet, Illinois
74 miles (total miles – 337)
Partly sunny, 70 degrees, with a slight tailwind

Peter

At the recommendation of our host, Rod, we sleep in a bit and waited until 9 a.m. to leave for downtown Chicago and the official beginning of historic Route 66. Apparently, there is a rush hour on the bike trail as well.

Before we leave, I do my daily basic bicycle safety check, the ABC Quick Check. A is for air. B is for brakes. C is for cranks, chain, and cogs. Quick, is for quick releases (wheels and seat(s), and Check is for a quick checkout ride.

I started following this routine years ago when I was a bicycle cop and it was required. Later, I taught the ABC Quick Check to hundreds of cyclists as a bicycle safety instructor for the League of American Bicyclists. I have discovered numerous mechanical issues such as flat and low tires, loose handlebars, disconnected or broken brakes over the years. I do this check before every single ride – and it's a good thing, too!

While checking the rear brake, I notice it is rubbing on the wheel rim. Strange. Upon further investigation, Rod (who once worked for Cannondale and knows bikes) and I discover a "ding" in the rim, probably from a rock.

We agreed after further inspection that the wheel is safe to ride, so I open the break slightly to stop the rubbing and we are good to go.

Tracy
The ride into the Windy City (thankfully, not windy today) is only about five miles right down the Lake Front Trail. The trail is still busy, but it is a beautiful ride with amazing views of the lake to our left and the city to our right. We really enjoy the ride and easily get to Buckingham Fountain in Grant Park near our Route 66 starting point. The fountain is magnificent. One of the largest in the world, it shoots water 150 feet into the air. This morning, we decide to be tourists and spend the next couple of hours bicycling around the city to check it out. We head to Millennium Park to experience the Bean. Officially named Cloud Gate, it is a highly polished stainless-steel sculpture shaped like a giant bean. The Bean acts like a mirror and provides interesting views of the city, and tourists like us, in its reflection. Very cool.

Peter
Eventually, it is time to ride to the corner of Michigan Avenue and Adams Street, three blocks away, to find the official starting point of Route 66. We locate the "BEGIN HISTORIC ROUTE 66" sign high up on a light pole in the northwest corner of the intersection. We take several pictures in front of the

Our morning of being tourists included a stop in front of Cloud Gate ("the Bean") in Chicago's Millennium Park.

sign (including the one on the cover of this book) and then cross the street for a treat at Starbucks to celebrate making it this far. Yes, there are Starbucks everywhere. After our snack, we take a deep breath and briefly contemplate what is yet to come. We remount the bike. Here we go.

We head back toward Buckingham Fountain and the Lake Front Trail, where we turn south along the lake. Our planned ending point for the day is Joliet, Illinois, about fifty miles away.

Shortly after rejoining the trail, we hit one of the strangest detours I have ever ridden through, certainly with a fully loaded tandem. In the distance, I can see orange construction signs along the trail, although I cannot read them yet. I call the signs out to Tracy. I know she cannot see them because I block her view, but I need her to be aware of what is coming up, just in case. As we get closer, I can see that the signs read "DETOUR AHEAD" with pictures of a bicyclist and a pedestrian.

"I wonder what that means?" I think to myself.

We continue along the trail a short distance until we come to a three-way intersection. The trail to the left, toward the lake, is blocked by a sawhorse and a "TRAIL CLOSED" sign. The trail to the right will take us to a busy signalized intersection, and presumably onto the road. The last option, marked by an orange "DETOUR" sign, continues straight ahead and is the most intriguing. This trail connects to a ramp, which goes up and into the second story of what looks like a parking garage.

"Really? The detour goes up there?" I say to myself.

Unsure of where to go, I call out to Tracy, "Where should I go?"

She calls back, "I don't know, I can't see!"

Great! I choose door number two and head up the ramp and into the parking garage.

It is hard to see inside the building at first as my eyes struggle to adjust to the relative darkness. All I can see are two yellow lines on the concrete floor that I presume mark the edges of the detour route.

"Can you see anything?" I yell.

All I get back is, "No!"

Just as I am about to stop to get my bearings, the two yellow lines abruptly angle to the right and then back to the left. I deftly rock the bike right then left to stay between the lines, with Tracy blindly following my lead, and narrowly miss a huge concrete support pillar to our left.

"Damn, that was close!"

As I prepare to stop again, the room opens up, light begins to stream in from the now-open sides of the building, and several cyclists appear in the distance coming toward us.

"This really is a detour. Go figure."

We greet the passing cyclists as though we ride this detour all the time, continue to the far side of the garage, ramp back down to the trail, and continue on our way. We are not at all sure what just happened. All we know is it worked, and we won't be going back that way.

We followed Old Plank Road Trail for much of the day on our ride from Chicago to Joliet, Illinois.

Tracy

We follow the Lakefront Trail to the South Chicago Neighborhood, where we hop on the Burnham Greenway Trail. Just outside the city of Chicago Heights, we join the Old Plank Road Trail for twenty-two more miles into the city of Joliet (pop. 147,433).

Most of our riding today is on trails, but unlike yesterday, there is only one trail to choose from and it is well marked. Although, there is still a fair amount of starting and stopping.

We meet a nice young couple bicycling on the trail just outside of Joliet. They are very interested in our trip, and the young man's mouth drops when we tell him how far we are going. It is so funny; he is totally speechless. We would love to talk longer, but we need to get to town and find a place to stay. It is already close to 7 p.m. I think we spent too much time in Chicago!

Peter

Just as we enter the Joliet city limits, Tracy thinks she hears a rubbing noise coming from the rear wheel. Oh, oh! That sounds familiar.

We stop along the side of a quiet residential street to check things out. Much to our dismay, I discover that the metal rear rim has a one-inch split running lengthwise and is slightly bowed. This must be what was causing the brake to rub this morning, and now it is much worse. We cannot fix this on the road if it gets any worse! It turns out the boys at the bike shop at home were right: I should have replaced our aged wheels before the trip. I guess 60,000 miles, much of it loaded touring, is the limit.

I tell Tracy I think the wheel is rideable. Probably. Being so close to town, I think we have a shot at making it to someplace safe before the wheel completely fails. Pushing the bike always sucks and trying to find a vehicle to transport it is a challenge.

"Is it safe?" she asks.

Since it is the rear wheel and not involved in steering the bike, I tell her that if the rim does completely fail and the wheel collapses while we are riding, all that will happen is that she will suddenly find herself much closer to the ground and we will unceremoniously grind to a halt.

"Okay," she says, looking at me skeptically.

We gingerly remount the bike and start to ride, doing our best to keep our speed down and avoid any unnecessary bumps. Tracy, the tent, and our two large panniers sit directly over the rear wheel. That's a lot of weight – sorry again, Honey! We limp our way to Harrah's Casino and Hotel, the closest lodging to us, but there is no room at the inn. Three more sketchy miles down the road, we find the Clarion Hotel and a room. It is now 7:30 p.m. and we are hungry, but we are safe and have a line on a bicycle shop, just one mile away. We walk to a Bob Evans chain restaurant for dinner, and then call it a night.

That was an interesting day. Tomorrow, we will unload the bike and ride, again gingerly, to the bicycle shop and see about a repair. We will probably be stuck here for a while. I am sure a new rim will need to be ordered and overnighted to us, if the bike shop can build us a new wheel.

Day 6
June 8 – Joliet, Illinois
1 mile (total miles – 338)
78 degrees and sunny

Tracy

We are spending today, and probably tomorrow, in Joliet. It is nice to get a break from biking and catch up a bit, even though we have only been on the

---

Kat's update to our followers

We Bike Route 66 - NEWS FLASH!
Mechanical failure temporarily halts Fluckes' progress.

After successfully making it to Chicago, IL, and the official starting point of Route 66 today, the Fluckes are temporarily stuck in Joliet, IL, after the rim of their rear wheel split. There was no crash involved and the Fluckes were able to ride the bike to a Joliet hotel. They will further assess the damage and their options tomorrow. Stay tuned for further updates.

Dawn N Hal Goodman (Bay Shore Bicycle Club members, Green Bay)
Good luck...get some rest...Wednesday is a whole new day.

Peter Flucke
We're good! Thanks Dawn.

Peter crosses his fingers as we hope the guys at Sunbaum Cycle in Joliet, Illinois, can fix the rear wheel of our bike.

road for five days. Normally, we try to ride for at least six days in a row and then take one day off. But things break and need to be taken care of.

Peter

Our number one priority for today is to see if we can get the bike fixed. No bike, no more bicycle trip. The good news is that Sunbaum Cycle is only one mile away from our hotel, easily rideable, or walkable if need be. The bad news is that the bicycle shop does not open until 10 a.m., and I have been awake since 5 a.m. So much for sleeping in. I am too worried to sleep.

As I lay in bed, I think about how things will play out at the bicycle shop. Most bicycle shops are pretty good about prioritizing repairs for touring cyclists. As cyclists themselves, they realize the bicycle is our only means of transportation and we are stuck without it. The bigger problem is likely to be the wheel itself. Tandem wheels, particularly the rear, are designed to carry a lot of weight and take an enormous amount of abuse. This is even truer for a touring tandem with the extra load. The hub on a rear tandem wheel is generally beefier. The rim is stronger and they usually have more spokes, forty in our case verses thirty-six on most bikes. It is common to have to special order parts. Further complicating the matter is Violet's age, sixteen years. Do they still make the parts we need? Do I need to buy a whole new wheel? What will that cost? Can we reuse the hub? How about the spoke length? Do we need a tandem-specific rim? Is that even a thing? I am way over my head here. What time is it?

I finally decide I need help and resolve to give JB Cycle & Sport, our bicycle shop at home, a call before we go to Sunbaum Cycle. They know our bike inside and out, and have replaced almost every part on it (except the wheels) over its 60,000-mile life, give or take a few miles. Unfortunately, JB Cycle does not open until 10 a.m. either. The call will make us a bit late for Sunbaum's opening, but we will be much better prepared when we get there.

At 10 a.m. on the dot, I call JB Cycle. No answer! Okay, they are probably outside putting out the display bikes. Then at 10:05 a.m., I get an answer.

"JB Cycle, this is Jeff."

Thank God! I have known Jeff Wentworth since 1993, when Tracy and I moved to the Green Bay area and I was starting our consulting business, WE BIKE, etc., LLC. Jeff was the manager/mechanic at another bicycle shop at the time, and I stopped in trying to sell him a copy of a statewide bicycle event calendar I had hand-typed at my kitchen table while watching our three-year-old. Jeff saw the value in the project and bought a few copies. Jeff opened his own bike shop a few years later and we rode thousands of miles together, most of them during early morning Saturday group road rides. I purchased most of our bicycles from Jeff and he maintained them all until he retired recently.

I explain our situation to Jeff, whereupon he says, "I told you, you should have replaced those rims before you left."

"You've got me there," I reply, thoroughly humbled.

Jeff tells me to see if Sunbaum can reuse the existing Hadley hub and build us a new wheel.

"That hub is bomb-proof," he says. "It should outlive you and your kids."

Okay, keep the hub. "What about the rim and the spokes?" I ask.

"I like Velocity rims, and the spokes shouldn't be a problem," he says.

"Thanks, I owe you."

"No problem. Have fun."

Boy, do I feel better!

Carefully, we ride the bike to Sunbaum Cycle, arriving at about 10:30 a.m. Per our custom, Tracy holds the door and I wheel the bike through. If I try and get the bike through the door myself, it invariably slams on the frame or back wheel, which would be adding insult to injury in this case.

Things start looking up the second we walk into the bike shop. We are the

This is us with Jeff, our hero at Sumbaum Cycle in Joliet, Illinois.

only ones there besides the medium-built, thirty-something guy with short, dark hair in the back who is working on a bike. The mechanic, Jeff (another good sign), introduces himself and asks how he can help us. We explain our predicament.

"We are stuck in town if we can't get it fixed," I say as pathetically as possibly.

"You want to keep that hub, right?" Jeff asks. Now we are in business.

"I'd sure like to," I say. "That thing should outlive our children."

He agrees. "I usually use Velocity rims," Jeff says.

Perfect!

"When do you want the new wheel by?" Jeff asks.

"As soon as possible," I reply.

"I have another repair ahead of you, and I'll have to order the rim and some spokes, but I should have them by tomorrow and I should have it done by Friday."

Two days in town, and we need a day off anyhow. Not bad for an epic lapse of judgement on my part.

"That will be great," I say. "Thank you."

"No problem, I'll give you a call when it's done."

And all is right with the world.

Tracy

After dropping off the tandem at the Sunbaum Cycle for repairs, we take an Uber (our first time) to downtown Joliet. The area is nice, but like many downtowns, it is struggling. Although, it does appear the city is working hard to revitalize it. Major infrastructure improvements including narrower

---

Kat's update to our followers

We Bike Route 66 - NEWS FLASH Update!

Early this afternoon, the Fluckes were able to ride their tandem bicycle with the split rear rim, one mile, to Sunbaum Cycle in Joliet, IL. (According to their website, Sunbaum is the second-oldest bicycle shop in the country - 1894.) There, they were able to order a new rim and spokes which mechanic ("wrench") Jeff will use to build a new wheel. The Fluckes hope to be back on the road by Friday afternoon.

---

streets, sidewalks, and lighting, along with public art, benches, street trees, wayfinding signage, and historical amenities have been added. Now they just need to entice businesses to come back.

While walking through downtown, I overhear an employee from the local economic development department talking with a potential developer. She is explaining that they have tax credits for new businesses looking to renovate an existing business. Great idea!

We explore the Route 66 Welcome Center, Joliet Historical Museum, Rialto Square Theater, and have lunch at the Chicago Street Pub. The farmers market is open, so we pick up dinner and take Uber back to our hotel for the evening.

Day 7
June 9 – Joliet, Illinois
1 mile (total miles – 339)
Cloudy and 72 degrees

Peter

Today we aren't going anywhere until the bike is fixed, so we sleep in, have a leisurely breakfast, work on social media, and walk to the post office to mail home our beer glass from Cedarburg, Wisconsin, and some receipts. Next, we walk to the nearby Bob Evans Restaurant for a late lunch and then head back to the hotel. At 4 p.m., much to our surprise, the bike shop calls. The tandem has a new rear wheel and is ready to go, and in record time.

We walk the mile to the bike shop, pay for the repairs ($322), thank Jeff the mechanic repeatedly, and ride triumphantly back to the hotel. Total miles for the day, one!

We eat dinner in our hotel room, pack and go to bed early, for tomorrow we ride!

Day 8
June 10 – Joliet to Dwight, Illinois
48 miles (total miles – 387)
Hot, 94 degrees, sunny with a 15-mph headwind

Tracy

Thanks to Jeff at Sunbaum Cycle, we are able to continue our trip this morning. We have a short day planned because we thought we would not have the bike back until noon and it is supposed to be hot with a strong headwind.

Peter

It is already 80 degrees outside when we leave the hotel at about 9 a.m. We head south along historic Route 66/STH 53. While the road may be historic, it kind of sucks to bike on, as it is narrow, high speed (55 mph), and has lots of trucks. It certainly is not the worst road we have ridden, but it could sure use a shoulder.

Tracy

This is the first time we are traveling on actual Route 66. The route takes us by some unique natural areas as well as manmade attractions. The first city we hit is Elwood. Elwood was the inspiration for Elwood Blues from the movie *The Blues Brothers* (1980), one of my favorite movies. Incidentally, the famous chase scene where the Pinto-driving Illinois Nazis drive off the end of a freeway ramp was shot in Milwaukee on the Daniel Hoan Memorial Bridge. The "Bridge to Nowhere" is about ten miles from my childhood home.

Just outside Elwood, we visit the Abraham Lincoln National Cemetery. Lincoln enacted a law

This Gemini Giant, also known as a "Muffler Man," greeted us in Wilmington, Illinois. These statues were used to encourage travelers to stop at local businesses in the 1960s.

creating national cemeteries in 1862 in the midst of the Civil War. This cemetery was created in 1999 on the grounds of an old munitions plant. Ironic! It is amazing to ride through this 982-acre site with grave stones as far as the eye can see. It is a beautiful and solemn place. Very moving. Twenty-eight funerals are scheduled on this day. The cemetery is open to all honorably discharged military members and their spouses.

Upon leaving the cemetery, we enter the Midewin National Tallgrass Prairie, where buffalo have recently been reintroduced. The prairie was established in 1996, covers 18,226 acres, and is managed by the US Department of Agriculture Forest Service. Sadly, we see no buffalo, just lots of cars and trucks.

Our next stop is the city of Wilmington, where we see our first "Muffler Man," the Gemini Giant. Muffler Men are large statues that were used in the 1960s to entice travelers to stop at local businesses. This particular statue was used to get people to eat at the now-closed Launching Pad restaurant. The 438-pound, thirty-foot-tall green Gemini Giant wears a space helmet and holds a rocket ship. The statue was created during the space race era and named after America's second space program, Project Gemini.

> ## Facebook followers
>
> **Dawn N Hal Goodman**
> Ride On, Safe journey, stay cool!
>
> **Peter Flucke**
> 90 degrees with an 11 mph headwind in Gardner, IL, but we are taking it easy and doing well. We are practicing for when it really gets hot. Lol

Next up is Braidwood and the famous 1950s Polk-a-Dot Drive In. This icon houses tons of Route 66 memorabilia. We do not stop in, however, because the place is extremely busy with a motorcycle group of about thirty. We have been crossing paths with them most of the day.

Peter

Our last thirteen miles to Dwight are tough! By this point in the day, the temperature is up to 94 degrees and the wind is blowing at 15 mph, right into my face. As hot as it is for me, it must be even worse for Tracy. I block the wind so she does not even have the full effect of the breeze to cool her off. We are riding on Route 66, adjacent to I-55 now. The road is quiet and in good shape, but unfortunately there is nothing to block the relentless headwind. Mercifully, the road is flat, but we can still only manage 10-12 mph. Eventually, we make it to the Super 8 hotel in Dwight (pop. 4,051) and are very pleased to discover that our room is an icebox. We ultimately have to turn the air conditioning off to keep from freezing.

Tracy

Peter is craving chocolate milk when we arrive in Dwight, so we walk to a convenience store where we find a big jug, along with some string cheese and a giant pickle. We must be craving protein and salt. I wonder why? After a nap, with our jackets on, we find some dinner and call it an early night. We are expecting the same headwinds and heat tomorrow, so we are going to try and be on the road at sunrise. We have approximately fifty-eight miles to ride tomorrow to Bloomington.

Day 9
June 11 – Dwight to Bloomington, Illinois
58 miles (total miles – 445)
Sunny, 94 degrees, with a 15-mph headwind

Tracy

We are up early and on the road by 7:30 a.m. It is going to be another hot day with a nasty headwind.

Our first stop is the small town of Odell, where we find a beautifully re-stored Standard Oil gas station. The station was built in 1932 and is on the National Register of Historic Places. It now serves as a visitor center, but is closed due to the early hour. It does have a nice, recorded message that tells the history of the site. They must have put in the recording for early-morning cyclists trying to beat the heat.

"Contractor Patrick O'Donnell purchased a small parcel of land along Route 66 in Odell, Illinois. He built a gas station there based on a 1916 Standard Oil of Ohio design, known as a domestic-style gas station. This 'house with canopy' style of gas station gave customers a comfortable feeling they could associate with home. This association created an atmosphere of trust for commercial and recreational travelers of the day."
(https://www.nps.gov/nr/travel/route66/standard_oil_gas_station_odell.html)

Julian and Noha provided our Warmshowers stay in Bloomington, Illinois. We have enjoyed visiting with them since this trip as well.

Peter

With the heat and the wind today, the going is slow. Our speed so far is hovering between 9 and 14 mph. Fortunately, there are several small towns along the route. Odell, Pontiac, Lexington, and Towanda, are fairly evenly spaced at eight to ten miles apart. Our plan is to ride from one town to the next, take a break somewhere with air conditioning, food, and water, and when our core temperatures return to something near normal, strike out again.

Tracy

In Pontiac, we find a cute little bakery with air conditioning. The down-town square has lots of historic buildings and some amazing murals. It is really nice here. The murals were painted by a traveling professional group and depict Route 66 attractions in the area. Word is there are also three old pedestrian swing bridges nearby that cross the Vermillion River. We only see one bridge, but immediately understand why the city is so proud of them. With its iron superstructure, cables, and narrow wooden walkway, it has character.

Our last twenty miles are tough. Even with frequent breaks, the heat and wind are seemingly sending us backwards at times. We are very glad to get to Bloomington and a cold beer at their local microbrewery.

Peter

When we finally make it to Bloomington (pop. 78,343), we stop at DES-TIHL Restaurant & Brew Works for a snack, a pint, and a glass. Shortly after we are seated by the host, we are completely surprised when a young woman walks up to us and says, "Hi, Mr. and Mrs. Flucke."

"Hello, Melissa. What are you doing here?" I ask.

Melissa Matheys is an elementary and high school friend of our oldest daughter, also named Melissa. Small world. When the girls were little, we called them M and M, and the girls had matching stretch pants and T-shirts with pictures of the M&M candy characters on them. So cute. Melissa M. now lives nearby.

From the restaurant, we take the Centennial Trail three miles to our Warmshowers stay for the night.

Tracy

Julian and Noha are there to greet us and show us where to secure the tandem for the night. As we are making room in the bicycle shed, we see their tandem, which looks very different than ours. Julian is a mountain of a man and Noha is tiny. Therefore, their custom-built Bilenky cockpits are very different in size (XXL/M). Since Peter and I are comparable in size (my legs and arms are actually longer than his), our cockpits are similar (L/M) and we could switch positions if needed. Noha could never captain their bike.

Julian and Noha both teach political science at Illinois State University in Normal and are experienced tandem riders. They have traveled extensively in other countries and have amazing stories to tell us. They make us a great dinner and we stay up chatting until late.

(We have kept in touch with Julian and Noha, and had the pleasure of spending time with them at the 2022 Midwest Tandem Rally in Decatur, Illinois. They have been great supporters of us and our first book, *Coast to Coast on a Tandem*.)

Peter

Tomorrow it will be hot again, but this time we will have a tailwind for the seventy miles to Springfield, our stopping point for the night. The tailwind should leave us with some time to explore this interesting city.

Day 10
June 12 – Bloomington to Springfield, Illinois
71 miles (total miles – 516)
Sunny, 90 degrees, with a 10-15-mph tailwind

Tracy

We wake up to slightly cooler temperatures and a tailwind. Yay! After a nice breakfast with Julian and Noha, Julian rides with us out of town. Finding our way back to our route in the mornings in a strange city can be a struggle. We greatly appreciate Julian's assistance. Stress-free navigating for me.

Our first stop for the day is Funks Grove, a stand of old-growth sugar maple trees. We bicycle the two-mile entrance road through a forest of magnificent gentle giants that dead ends at the Sugar Bush Nature Center. With a love of all things tree, and a degree in forestry to match, Peter is in his glory. The nature center is closed, but we still enjoy exploring the grounds.

"Can you believe the size of those maple logs?" Peter keeps saying (over and over again).

Peter

When it is time to head back to Route 66, we ride to the turnaround just past the nature center instead of going back the way we had come. Last night, Julian had told us about a shortcut over some railroad tracks behind the nature center where we could sneak back to Route 66. This little maneuver will save us about four miles. Sounds like it is worth a try.

There is a ditch followed by a ten-to-fifteen-foot embankment next to the turnaround, which leads to the railroad tracks. Both are steep, and covered in brush and weeds. The tracks are just barely visible at the top of the hill and we almost do not see them.

"You think this is where we are supposed to go?" I ask Tracy.

"I'm not sure," she says. "Let me climb up there and take a look while you hold the bike."

"Okay with me," I think to myself. "That looks like ragweed."

Tracy fights her way along what seems like it might be a footpath and calls back from the top.

"Yup, this is it. I'm on the tracks and I can see the highway on the other side. I think we can make it."

"Do we need to take the bags off the bike?" I ask.

"No, I think we can leave them on."

We both ease the bike down into the ditch, and then throw our weight into it and just barely make it up the steep incline. We are both covered in pickers, but we made it. (Kind of reminds me of being a park ranger.) Now all we have to do is get a fully loaded tandem over the tracks and down the other side safely.

As we struggle to negotiate the rails without dumping the bike, we notice a headlight on the tracks in the distance to our right.

"What do you think that is?" I ask Tracy.

"IT'S A TRAIN!" she yells back.

Julian had told us that the railroad has been improving the tracks in the area for HIGH-SPEED trains. Could this be one of them? Oh, $#!+! WE NEED TO MOVE!

We summon superhuman strength and get the bike, bags, and ourselves over the tracks without incident and are soon back on good old Route 66. As we continue down the road, we do see a train on the tracks with its headlight on, but it is only idling, not moving. The joke was on us! Better safe than sorry.

Tracy

With the wind at our backs, we zoom through the next fifteen miles and then stop for a quick early lunch in Atlanta (pop. 1,637, much smaller than Atlanta, Georgia.) Yesterday, we were averaging about 10 mph into the head-wind and today we are at about 17 mph with the tailwind. The restaurant we stop at is nice, but the service is very slow. Our short stop turns into an hour. Across the street from the restaurant, we see our second Muffler Man, "Tall Paul," a nineteen-foot statue of a man holding a hotdog.

The wind stays behind us, but it is getting hotter and we make frequent stops in more little towns like Lincoln, Broadwell, Elkhart, Williamsburg, and Sherman to fill our water bottles, get a snack, and stand in the air conditioning.

We talked on the phone with our youngest daughter, Alexandra, earlier today and she was teasing us about the heat we are experiencing, saying it is nothing compared to where she lives in southern Texas. Sassy child, we will be there soon enough.

It is early afternoon when we reach Springfield (pop. 116,565), so we decide to stop at Obed & Isaac's Microbrewery & Eatery to see what they have to offer. After a beer and a snack, we bike the mile and a half to our Warmshowers stay for the night.

Our host for the evening is a very interesting young Chinese man, Yong Wu. He is a traveler himself and likes to host others to repay the kindnesses he has experienced. Yong is also hosting two young men from China this evening at his home, definitely a bachelor pad. Both men started in San Francisco and have been bicycling the United States for the past four months. They are headed to Chicago, where one will fly home and the other will continue on. One of the gentlemen speaks and understands a bit of English, but the other does not speak or understand English at all. They are very lucky to have Yong as their host, because he speaks Chinese.

Yong's family owns a Chinese restaurant nearby, so he picks up supplies and makes an amazing Chinese barbecue dinner for all of us. He is a great cook and we all stuff ourselves. Dinner is fun and a wonderful chance to get to know each other better. It is another fun night with a very welcoming host.

Day 11
June 13 – Springfield to Staunton, Illinois
68 miles (total miles – 584)
Sunny, 94 degrees, with a light headwind

Tracy

Springfield is a beautiful city and we are looking forward to seeing more of it on our ride out of town.

We leave early, hoping to miss rush hour traffic, which we do. I am not sure they have much of a rush hour here, since it seems like a sleepy place. We bicycle right past the state capitol building. It is very impressive and has a cool statue of Abraham Lincoln out front.

As we pedal by the capitol, all I can think about is the extreme financial problems Illinois is currently experiencing. The state has not passed a budget in several years, and it sounds like some major changes will need to occur to get it done. Several state parks have already been closed, and one of our Warm Shower hosts told us they may have to close the public school their children attend. Very sad. Hopefully the governor and legislatures can find a way to work together for the benefit of all.

We stop at Starbucks for breakfast, and as we are waiting in line to order, a gentleman about our age comes into the restaurant and approaches us. He asks if he can take a picture of our bicycle to put up on his website/blog that features cross-country bicyclists. He and his friend had seen us negotiating city traffic on the tandem, and figured we knew what we were doing. We say, "Sure," hand him our business card, and tell him we are posting to Facebook and blogging about our trip if he wants to follow us.

He says, "Great," and leaves to take the picture and talk with his buddy. The man comes back a few minutes later and asks if he can join us at our table as his friend had to leave. "Of course."

Ivan Wright is a former law enforcement officer (like Peter), a law enforcement instructor at the local college, and a hardcore bicyclist. His friend knows Peter because Peter was the instructor for a bicycling class the friend took in Milwaukee several years ago. Too funny. First Melissa Matheys in Bloomington and now one of Peter's students. It certainly is a small world.

After an enjoyable visit with Ivan, we head to the Interurban Trail that takes us about ten miles to the village of Chatham. The trail is well-maintained and easy to ride.

After Chatham, we mainly bicycle on original Route 66. It is pretty cool because cities have started posting the year in which each piece of highway was built. Route 66 has had many alignments over the years due to construction issues, and of course, politics. Today we travel on many miles of roadway built between 1930 and 1940. Most of the road is in good shape, but we do have a few sections that are really bad. They shake us up good!

Some of the newer road sections still have the older road adjacent to it. Although the older road tends to be in very bad shape and unusable, several

---

Facebook posts related to meeting Ivan

Peter Flucke is at Starbucks (Springfield, Illinois)
Another small world moment, just ran into an ex-cop in Springfield who is a biking buddy of a guy I trained in a biking class in Milwaukee years ago. He was very pleased with how Tracy and I negotiated city traffic on the tandem - glad we did it right!

Jim Baross Jr. (National bicycle safety instructor)
Of course you did it right!

Peter Flucke
Not an easy task with a fully loaded tandem and 2"+ parallel cracks between lanes - same stuff, different day and city. Sad that one needs this level of skill to pull this off!

Jim Baross Jr.
Ride on... and overcoming obstacles is likely part of why you/we do this stuff.

Peter Flucke
So true!

Adam Clayton (Professional Planning Engineer)
At least you know your training is being followed by others. I would be concerned if they thought you were doing it wrong!

Ivan's post about meeting us

Ivan Wright is at Starbucks (Springfield, Illinois)
This is the setup of long distance riders I met this morning. Just love the water supply. Earlier today at Starbucks on Stevenson Drive. http://www.webike.org/

---

cities are renovating these pieces and building bicycle paths. We have heard that the state would like to construct a bicycle path along their entire section of Route 66. They already have a good start on it, and we see several more areas under construction. We do wonder, though, where the money is coming from for the projects. It might be federal multimodal dollars, or possibly money earmarked specifically for Route 66 projects.

Peter

Springfield, Chatham, Divernon, Farmersville, Waggoner, Litchfield, Mount Olive, and Staunton, lots of small towns again today.

In Mount Olive, we find an old Shell gas station to check out. We cannot get inside, but the outside is beautifully restored. Soulsby's Service Station

Henry Soulsby built Soulsby's Service Station in 1926 after he learned Route 66 would be coming through Mount Olive, Illinois. It is now on the National Registry of Historic Places.

was built in 1926 by Henry Soulsby of Mount Olive. A former miner like his father before him, an injury forced Soulsby into a new line of work. When he found out Route 66 would come through Mount Olive, he bought property on a corner of 1st Street (now Old Route 66) and built a gas station to serve the anticipated flood of tourists. Built in the house and canopy style, the station's design was intended to blend in with the existing neighborhood and thus avoid the "crudeness" associated with gas stations. The station stopped selling gas in 1991, closed its doors for good in 1993, and was sold in 1997. The current owner and the Soulsby Preservation Society started restoring the station in 2003, and it was placed on the National Registry of Historic Places the following year.

The string of small towns works well with how the day is playing out. It is another hot one, but we are handling it well. Our strategy of drinking lots of water, biking until we start to overheat, and then ducking into an air-conditioned convenience store to cool off seems to be working.

I know from experience that when I start to get what I call a "heat headache," it is time for me to get somewhere cool. The heat headache seems to be my first symptom of heat exhaustion and it is not to be ignored. I have tried to push through this headache a couple of times over the years with the same results every time: I get really sick. Heat exhaustion can quickly progress to heat stroke if not treated.

I treated a number of people for heat stroke on very hot summer days when I was a Minnesota Park Ranger and Emergency Medical Technician (EMT). Confusion-altered mental status, slurred speech, hot, dry skin or profuse sweating, very high body temperature, and seizures are all signs of heat stroke, which can be fatal if treatment is delayed. Fortunately, Tracy and I can monitor each other for problems. It is one of the many advantages of riding tandem. When I start to get grumpy, when Tracy starts to struggle with navigation, or when I complain of a headache, it is time to find some shade. Either one of us can call for a break at any time. No questions asked. At the suggestion of our biking friend, Peggy Olson, I have started taking refuge in convenience store walk-in beer coolers from time to time. No one seems to mind. Nice!

Tracy

After another hot day on the bicycle, we are glad to get into Staunton (pop. 5,023) a bit early and recuperate. We stop at a Dairy Queen before going to our hotel for the night. I get a large malt, something I have been craving all day. It takes care of the craving and will probably hold me for the rest of the trip.

Peter

We are spending the night at a Super 8 in Staunton, which turns out to be a good idea. Besides the shower and air conditioning feeling GREAT, the skies just opened up and it would have been a rough night in the tent. Someone is definitely watching out for us.

Day 12
June 14 – Staunton, Illinois to Webster Groves, Missouri
58 miles (total miles – 642)
Sunny, 95 degrees, with a light headwind

Tracy

We get started a little later today because we are meeting a reporter in the town of Edwardsville, Illinois, to do a story about us for the *Edwardsville Intelligencer*. We are meeting him at 9 a.m. and only have eighteen miles to cover to get there. The ride is really nice, and pretty much all on the Madison County Transit (MCT) Quercus Grove Trail. Madison County builds and maintains the trail system, and they have done a great job.

Nine miles from Edwardsville, we spy a fellow bicycle tourist coming toward us. The bags on his bicycle and his weathered look are a dead giveaway. As per tradition, the cyclist and Peter both raise a hand in the air indicating a willingness to stop and chat. He swings his bicycle to the shoulder on our side of the trail. The thirty-something rider is from Columbia and is doing Route 66 from west to east. We exchange information about what to expect up the road. I think he is smarter than us riding west to east with the prevailing westerly winds pushing him along. We wish each other well and head our separate ways.

We arrive in Edwardsville right on time and spend about a half hour with Steve Horrell, the reporter, and his photographer, Zachery. Steve has some great questions for us and we truly enjoy the interview, and apparently Steve does as well. (A month or so after we finish our trip, Steve contacts us to see if we will do a Skype interview with a journalism class he is teaching at the local college. He thought it would be great for the students to hear about our adventure, ask questions, and then write an article about the interview. We agreed and in August did the interview. We thoroughly enjoyed working with the class, although they still have a long way to go to compete with Steve. He is a master.)

After breakfast in Edwardsville, we hop on the bicycle and head for St. Louis, Missouri.

We cross the Mississippi River into Missouri on the Old Chain of Rocks Bridge just downstream of the new Chain of Rocks Bridge, also known as I-270. The old bridge was built in 1929 to accommodate increased traffic over the river caused by Route 66. A unique feature of this bridge is the twenty-two-degree bend in the middle. The turn was due, in part, to navigational issues in the river channel below caused by an extremely hard rock ledge,

The mile-long Old Chain of Rocks Bridge was our entry to the state of Missouri over the Mississippi River on our way to St. Louis.

known as the Chain of Rocks. The bridge was closed in 1968 and scheduled for demolition in 1975. Luckily, the price for scrap metal was low at the time and the bridge remained standing. In 1999, a regional bicycle group lobbied to open it as a bicycle and pedestrian bridge, and the mile-long bridge has been available for this use ever since.

Peter

Last year, we bicycled through St. Louis on the Riverfront Trail while riding the length of the Mississippi River. Again, starting at our home in Green Bay, we first rode northwest to International Falls, Minnesota, on the Canadian border, and then headed south to Itasca State Park and the headwaters of the Mississippi River, which is really no more than a stream at that point. From there, we followed the river south as it grew larger and larger until we reached the Gulf of Mexico, ninety miles south of New Orleans, Louisiana. The Riverfront Trail was under construction the last time we passed through.

Tracy

We enter St. Louis (pop. 312,926) from the north on the Riverfront Trail, which drops us right at Gateway Arch National Park. It is amaz-

The Gateway Arch was a sight for sore eyes (and legs) when we arrived in the St. Louis area.

ing to see how much work has been completed on the trail since just last fall. It looks great.

Peter

The Gateway Arch is a sight to behold and has a special place in my heart. The 630-foot parabolic arch, top to bottom and leg to leg, was designed by Finnish-American architect Eero Saarinen and constructed from February 12, 1963, to October 28, 1965. The arch reflects St. Louis's role in the westward expansion of the United States in the nineteenth century.

My father's family is from the St. Louis area, and we often visited relatives there when I was growing up. My aunt, Lolly (Flucke) Wehrli, told me a story once about watching the arch being built and the day the two legs were joined at the top and the last piece of the skin was hammered into place. There is a unique pod-like tram inside the arch that takes visitors to the top, where one gets a commanding view of the city, countryside, and of course, the Mississippi River. Tracy and I have ridden the tram several times, but decide to skip it today as it is getting late.

Tracy

From the arch, we head west to hotel row. Our plan this morning was to ride to St. Louis and then find a room for the night. This is what we did on our Mississippi River bicycle trip, and we had our choice of where to stay. Not a great idea this time, as it turns out. Little did we know that there is a huge convention and a Cardinals baseball game happening tonight. Every room within a forty-five-mile radius is booked and there are no campgrounds. Oh, oh!

Peter and I often say that the difference between being a bicycle tourist and being homeless can be a very fine line.

(Several years ago, we got a call at home from a friend who was a hotel clerk in Green Bay. She explained that a touring bicyclist had stopped at the hotel to get a room for the night. Unfortunately, it was the day of the Green Bay Packers' stockholders meeting, and there was not a room available within a sixty-mile radius. She asked if we would be able to put him up for the night. We said "Sure" and told her to send him our way. Chris was from Illinois and was bicycling around Lake Michigan. He was thankful for the hospitality and told us he was planning to sleep on a park bench that night. His wife reached out a couple of days later to thank us for "saving her husband.")

Luckily, we had been planning to see Peter's cousin, Carol Wehrli, and possibly his Aunt Lolly, who live in Webster Groves, a suburb about ten miles to the west. I reach out to Carol, and she is kind enough to take in a couple of weary bicyclists for the night. Thank goodness. If Carol hadn't come through, I am not sure where we would have stayed. I don't think we have the energy or time to get far enough out of the city to find a room or campground. Lesson learned. Plan a bit better in the future.

Our route to Webster Groves (pop. 23,005) takes us on Highway 100/ Chouteau Avenue/Manchester Avenue, a large urban arterial road in a very large metropolitan area (pop. 2,198,000). Fortunately, the road is equipped with bicycle lanes, which made it easy to navigate, even at rush hour. The ride was almost enjoyable. We arrive at Carol's house within an hour, thankful for a safe place to rest our heads for the night.

Peter blends in nicely with the more historic figures depicted on one of the many building murals in Cuba, Missouri, the officially designated Route 66 Mural City.

Chapter 3

State of Missouri

June 15-20, 2016
420 miles/978 total

Day 13
June 15 – Webster Groves to Sullivan, Missouri
71 miles (total miles – 713)
Sunny, 94 degrees, with an 8-11-mph headwind

Tracy

Peter's cousin, Carol, is up early to make us coffee and see us off. The coffee is greatly appreciated. Thanks for everything, Carol.

Today is our sixth day on the road without a break and it is already warm, 78 degrees, as we leave at 6 a.m. It may prove to be a tough day with the expected hills and heat. Oh, well. With lots of water on board, we begin our trip.

Our ride starts in the west suburbs of St. Louis on Highway 100/Manchester Road. Unfortunately, the suburbs did not get it right for bicyclists

like they did in St. Louis. The ride is challenging due to the heavy traffic, construction, freeway interchanges, and lack of bicycle accommodations. They do have SHARE THE ROAD signs up, which probably help create an awareness and let motorists know a bicyclist has a right to be on the road. The thirteen miles to Ellisville are tough and take all our collective skill and nerve, but we make it.

Peter

The traffic starts to thin near Ellisville, but both the temperature and terrain are starting to climb. We are entering the Ozark Mountains, and we are a bit intimidated. This is the most extensive highland region between the Appalachian Mountains and Rockies, and we will be in the Ozarks through the southeastern corner of Kansas and into eastern Oklahoma. We are pleased, however, to discover that after so many days of flat roads, "We have legs," as cyclists like to say, and are handling the first moderate climbs with ease. At Eureka, we rejoin historic Route 66.

Many thanks to Nathan Vandervest, our trainer, and Lee Hyrkas, nutritionist, from Bellin Health in Green Bay for working with us to get into great shape and help us develop strategies for staying that way, even in these extreme conditions.

Tracy

It is beautiful in the Ozarks, and we can see forever at the top of the climbs. The roads are also lightly traveled, which is a welcome change. We stop for lunch in the city of St. Clair at the Lewis Café, which has been in business for seventy-two years. The café has great food and the staff is very friendly. Only fifteen miles to go to Sullivan, our ending spot for the night.

Peter

We are still climbing well; now all we have to do is deal with the heat (expected high of 94 degrees) and the infamous Missouri humidity.

For the rest of the day we are on historic Route 66, which serves here as the frontage road for I-44. Normally, this is not our favorite feature to ride along, although the highway does provide us with services every 8-12 miles. This allows us to cool off (more beer coolers to hide in), fuel up, and hydrate, hydrate, hydrate. We have been consuming a lot more water than usual lately because of the heat and hills, and this is a bit of a concern to us. Typically, we each use about one large bottle (24 oz.) of water per hour, supplemented with

Beer coolers provided welcome relief from the heat and humidity we encountered at many points in our trip. Here, Peter enjoys a break in Sullivan, Missouri.

a sports drink for the electrolytes. With six bottles on the bike, we can ride for about three hours before we need to fill up again. That means we can cover about forty-five miles if we average fifteen mph, which isn't always the case.

I have been using 1.5 or more bottles per hour of late, and Tracy just a little less than that. Effectively, our range before we need to find water has been cut by one-third to about thirty miles. This is not a concern for now with services every 8-12 miles, but as we continue to move west, that will likely change. To the west, we expect lower population densities and fewer towns, much more climbing (7,882 feet to our high point), and dry desert air. Water could become a significant issue.

With not much else to distract us from the oppressive heat along the highway, we have become fixated on the huge, omnipresent, billboards advertising Meramec Caverns in Stanton. We enjoy exploring caves, and they are a cool, 60 degrees. Also, we have heard a lot about the caverns from our St. Louis family. They are only one hour away by air-conditioned car. We should be able to make the last tour of the day if we can keep up our pace. From Stanton, we will only have nine miles left to ride for the day. The caverns will be a nice break. Unfortunately, when we arrive in Stanton, we discover the caverns are three miles off route. Three miles there and three miles back will equal six more miles in this heat. We just can't do it. Sadly, we take a quick break at a convenience store along the interstate, then continue on our way.

Our progress is slow but steady, and by 5 p.m. we make it to our hotel in Sullivan (pop. 7,101). At a nearby convenience store, chocolate milk and a pickle (think protein and sodium if the combination grosses you out) never tasted so good!

We still regret having to skip Meramec Caverns in Stanton, but we were just too pooped to ride the extra miles. The plan is to take tomorrow off to rest, relax, and tour the caverns. This sounds way better than trying to bike in the expected high temperature of 100 degrees.

Day 14
June 16 – Sullivan, Missouri
0 miles (total miles – 713)
Hot and humid, 100 degrees

Tracy

Today is a rest day. We sleep in (well, later than normal, 7:30 a.m.), hit the hotel breakfast, do laundry, purchase supplies, and catch up on our blog and other social media. Even though we have the day off, we are still busy preparing to continue the ride tomorrow.

We are also playing tourist, and late morning take an Uber to the Meramec

Caverns in Stanton. The caverns are cool, literally and figuratively. The temperature inside is 60 degrees compared to 100 degrees outside. The caverns were opened to the public in 1933, and it is said that Jesse James and his gang took refuge here in 1874 after robbing a train in Gadshill, Missouri.

Meramec Caverns is the largest cave west of the Mississippi. In 1720, Frenchman Philipp Renault was drawn to the site by an Osage Indian legend telling of "veins of glittering yellow metal." Upon entering the cave through a gaping fifty-foot-wide by twenty-foot-high hole in the bluff, the exploration party discovered the gold was actually saltpeter (or potassium nitrate). Potassium nitrate was a key ingredient for the manufacturing of gunpowder during the 144 years mining took place in the cave. Renault named the cave Saltpeter Cave.

Tracy takes advantage of the flat penny machine in the Meramec Caverns gift shop to collect a lightweight souvenir.

Lester Dill purchased the cave in 1933 and changed the name from Saltpeter Cave to Meramec Caverns, and quickly began promoting and offering tours to the public. (https://www.americascave.com/)

The cave tour was amazing, and the gift shop just inside the cave entrance was not bad either, although completely man-made. I was excited to see a flat penny machine in the gift shop. I have a flat (smashed) penny collection, and of course had to get one. Flat pennies are cool, no matter what Peter says, and are a low-cost, small, and lightweight souvenir. They are a good thing to collect on a cross-country bicycle trip, much better than beer glasses. Little known fact: There are over 3,300 penny press machines in the United States.

Day 15
June 17 – Sullivan to St. Robert, Missouri
73 miles (total miles – 786)
Sunny, 89 degrees, with a nice tailwind

Tracy

Today is a much better day to be on the bicycle. The humidity is lower, and the temperature has dropped into the high eighties. We laugh because we think it is so much cooler, and it still is in the upper eighties! This just goes to show what you can get used to.

We get up and going early, as has become our norm, to beat the heat, and we know we will have lots of hills to climb.

The first city we hit is Cuba. Cuba has been designated the Route 66 Mural City by the Missouri legislature in recognition of Viva Cuba's Outdoor Mural Project. The murals, which are painted on several buildings along Route 66, are amazing and add a little something to our ride. We come across the "World's Largest Rocking Chair" on the outskirts of Cuba.

Peter

Not all roadside attractions on historic Route 66 are, well, historic. The former "World's Largest Rocking Chair" in Cuba, Missouri, was built in 2008 by the nearby Route 66 Fanning Outpost solely for the purpose of breaking the Guinness World Record for large rocking chairs. Constructed of welded steel, the massive chair stands forty-two feet tall, twenty feet wide, weighs 27,500 pounds, and sports the outpost's logo. The record was supplanted by a chair in Casey, Illinois, in 2015. Since then, the Cuba chair has been repainted red and renamed the "Route 66 Red Rocker."

Tracy

We see lots of strange things along Route 66. It truly is an interesting place to explore. The people we have met so far have been friendly, and intrigued and excited about our trip.

The second half of the ride today is uphill, but the hills are not too bad. They are definitely less steep than the Green and White Mountains in the eastern United States, and shorter than the Cascades in the west.

We make it to St. Robert (pop. 6,095) by 2:30 p.m. It is nice to get in early after an easier day on the bicycle. Our last day on the bike (to Sullivan) was also about seventy miles, but between the headwind and heat, it took us almost eleven hours to get it done. Today was only eight hours on the bike. Yay!

St. Robert is the home of the Fort Leonard Wood Military Reservation. It is where my dad, Gilbert Meisner, did his army basic training. It is a huge facility. The town has lots of services for a community its size. The military population must help spur economic development. After Fort Leonard Wood, Dad was transferred to Camp McClellan (now Fort McClellan) in Anniston, Alabama, where he served for two years (1954-1956) in Battalion Supply. He secured supplies for one battalion, three companies. My dad does not talk about his military service much, so it was fun to have an excuse to ask him about it. Thank you for your service, Gilbert John Meisner, private first class!

Tomorrow, we climb again at the start of our day, then head downhill with one more climb to our end point.

Facebook post

Facebook-generated title:
Peter Flucke is eating Chinese at Ocean Buffet. – St. Robert, MO

Our fortune cookie says: "Be Patient! The Great Wall didn't get built in one day." So true!

Day 16
June 18 – St. Robert to Marshfield, Missouri
68 miles (total miles – 854)
Sunny, 89 degrees, with a tailwind

Peter

Our ride today has lots of ups and downs, literally. The terrain is very hilly with short climbs, long climbs, short downhill, and long downhills. The variety is nice and none of the hills are so steep or long that they are too challenging to get over.

We see three touring cyclists ahead of us as we are bicycling out of Waynesville, and of course we have to try and chase them down. When we finally catch up, we introduce ourselves to a young woman, her boyfriend, and father.

They are from Switzerland and have been bicycling since May 1. They will be completing their trip tomorrow in Springfield, Missouri. The trio started in Toronto, Canada (where the young woman recently graduated with her master's degree), bicycled to Duluth, Minnesota, and then headed south to Route 66 for the end of their trip.

We ride with them for a while and then take off on our own. We are typically much faster on a tandem than most cyclists on a single bike. We meet up with them again later at Click's Convenience Store near Hazelgreen. The Route 66 bridge near here is listed as being closed in the Adventure Cycling Association map addendum, and we need some local intel.

Tracy

We talk with several locals to find out if we can cross the bridge, or if indeed it is impassable. The young man from Switzerland talks with a local family in the parking lot while Peter and I check with the clerk in the store. The clerk is on the phone with her husband when we walk in. Together, they agree that the bridge is safe to cross, but only by foot or bicycle, and we will have to lift our bicycles over two guard rails.

Our new Swiss friends assist us in lifting our heavy ride over a set of guardrails so we can use this old Route 66 bridge rather than ride on I-44.

When we come back outside, the family offers us bicyclists a pint of fresh raspberries to eat. We happily accept and down all the berries in no time flat. They were delicious!

As a group, we decide to give the bridge a try and agree to help each other lift the bicycles over the guardrails. This is extremely important to us. Without help, we will have to remove all the bags and tent from the bicycle, lift everything over the first guardrail, put everything back on the bike, ride across the bridge, take everything off again, lift it all over the second rail, and then put it all back on the bike to continue our ride.

Our new friends are great, and between all of us we are able to lift all four bicycles, including the tandem, over the guardrail without removing a single bag. Nice! We take a bunch of pictures and then continue on our way. It has been fun to work with these kindred spirits and get to know them a bit.

It is especially nice to stay on route because otherwise we would have had to ride on the shoulder of I-44 for nine miles. Doable, but not much fun!

Peter

After a few miles, we say goodbye and thank you to the Swiss contingent and continue our ride alone. We see them later in the afternoon when they buzz by us while we are stopped for a break. Further down the road, we buzz by them when they are resting. Both times we just smile and wave.

The rest of the day is uneventful and we make it to our ending point of Marshfield (pop. 7,188) by early afternoon. This allows us to take a nice nap before getting organized for the next day.

As we are talking at dinner, we realize we have now met and cycled with bicyclists from Columbia, China, and Switzerland. Very cool!!

Day 17
June 19 – Marshfield to Springfield, Missouri
36 miles (total miles – 890)
Sunny, 89 degrees, with a slight headwind

Tracy

First, we want to wish our fathers and the father figures in our lives – Gil Meisner, Paul Flucke, and Rod Mackenzie – a very happy Father's Day. Thanks for always being there for us! Happy Father's Day to Peter and all the other dads as well.

Today is a short day and an easy ride to Springfield. We sleep in a bit later than usual and then head to the hotel lobby for breakfast. While we are eating, the three bicyclists from Switzerland (Nina, Christof, and Dominic) walk in. We enjoy breakfast with them and then we all hit the road for Springfield. This is their last day on the road and we can tell they are having mixed feelings about being to the end. We remember that feeling from our past two trips. On the one hand, we were glad to have accomplished what we set out to do, but on the other, we were sad it was over. We have enjoyed meeting them.

We arrive in Springfield (pop. 166,715) at about 11:30 a.m. and go to the Springfield Brewing Company for lunch and a beer. Of course. We then bicycle across town to check out the 1902 Jefferson Avenue Footbridge. Crossing thirteen railroad tracks, it is one of the longest pedestrian bridges in the United States. Unfortunately, the walkway is closed for safety inspections. Oh well, it is cool to see anyway. Next, we head to downtown Springfield to

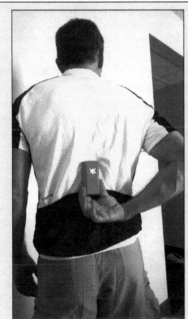

Kat's update to our followers

Wondering exactly where Peter and Tracy Flucke are on their We Bike Route 66 Bicycle Adventure? Go to (a now-inactive link) to find out. Where are they tonight? Otherwise, Peter has been carrying this tracking device in his back pocket for two weeks for nothing. Enjoy!

Tracy, with our GoPro camera on her helmet, poses in front of the Jefferson Avenue Footbridge in Springfield, Missouri, one of the longest pedestrian bridges in the United States. Unfortunately, it was closed for inspections when we were in town.

check out the public square in the middle of downtown. The square is basically a small park with lots of green space, and places to sit and relax. Unfortunately, the downtown is really struggling and there is not much else to see or do here. Our next stop is Mother's Brewery, where we have a beer, buy our second beer glass for the day, and then head over to our Warmshowers stay.

Our Warmshowers host, Dale, was born and raised in the city. He explains that the downtown has been in decline for many years. The city is really trying to revitalize it, but it has been tough, and the businesses and people just are not coming back. It is sad to see these downtown areas in cities deteriorating so much.

Dale is an amazing host. He is planning his own cross-country ride, so he peppers us with questions about our bicycle, gear, and anything else he can think of. We are happy to help in any way we can. Dale is a massage therapist and gives Peter a much-needed massage. Apparently, he does this with all of his guests. We have a delicious dinner and Dale makes us feel like family.

We turn in early because tomorrow we have another long day. We are heading to Carthage, eighty-eight miles away.

Day 18
June 20 – Springfield to Carthage, Missouri
88 miles (total miles – 978)
Sunny, 95 degrees, with a light headwind

Tracy

After a wonderful early-morning homemade breakfast with Dale, we all head off on our bikes. Dale is riding with us the first twenty miles to the town of Halltown. It is nice to have our host, who rides so well, lead us out of town and take us to Springfield's Birthplace of Route 66 Roadside Park. The park is cool, and we are glad to get a personal tour.

Peter

Springfield is the official birthplace of Route 66. In 1926, businessmen John T. Woodruff of Springfield and Cyrus Avery of Oklahoma first proposed US 66 as the name of the new highway in a telegram from a meeting of highway officials at the Colonial Hotel in Springfield.

Tracy

It is bittersweet to say goodbye to Dale in Halltown. After hugs, Dale heads back to Springfield and we continue to Carthage.

Our Adventure Cycling map shows limited services between Springfield and Carthage. There are many small towns along the route, with the town of Miller (pop. 685) being the biggest. Miller is the only community with services listed including a post office, convenience store, and restaurant. Hopefully, the restaurant will be open when we get there.

The first half of today's ride is very hilly, and of course, it is hot and there

Our Warmshowers host, Dale, gave us a personal tour of Springfield's Birthplace of Route 66 Roadside Park.

is a headwind. We are pooped by the time we hit the halfway point. The hills are particularly tough near Miller, and we are pleasantly surprised when we find the restaurant is open. Now we do not have to live on Clif Bars and trail mix, or worry about water for the rest of the ride.

Fortunately, the second half of the ride is much flatter and slightly down-hill. We are almost out of the Ozarks!

Peter

We are cruising right along now, but we need to find somewhere to stop and put on sunscreen, hopefully out of the direct sun. It has been quite some time since we have seen anything we would call shade. This is definitely the middle of nowhere.

Finally, we spot a lone building in the distance. The building looks like an old store or maybe even a saloon. As we approach, we can see that the first floor of two is raised several feet above the ground, and it has a porch. There are a couple of bicycles leaning against the front of the building and two young men are taking a nap in rickety old wooden chairs on the porch. I think we woke them up. Sorry guys!

We park the bike, introduce ourselves, and climb gratefully into the shade of the porch. The young men are also riding Route 66 and taking a much-needed break like us. One guy is from Ohio (Tyler) and the other is from China. They met along the route and decided to travel together to Santa Monica, California. We chat for a bit, put on our sunscreen, and then contin-ue on our way. Hopefully, we will run into Tyler and his companion again. It was a great boost to meet these fellow Route 66ers.

Tracy

After a long, hot day, we finally arrive in Carthage (pop. 14,654) about 4 p.m. We bicycle through the city to see the historic homes. There are four historic districts in the city with over 550 buildings listed on the National Registry of Historic Places, several dating back as far as 1888.

We promise ourselves to ride slowly back through the area in the morning and take it all in. Carthage also has, and boasts of, hundreds of mature maple trees. I totally understand why Carthage is known as America's Maple Leaf City.

We eat a quick dinner and then do our regular nightly chores (laundry, bike maintenance, posting to social media). Completely toasted from another long, hot day in the saddle, we pack it in early for the night.

Tomorrow will be another long, hot, windy one. Wish us luck!

We weren't in Kansas for long, but long enough to see the small town of Galena.

Chapter 4

State of Kansas

June 21, 2016
84 miles (Kansas - 13 miles)/1,062 total

Day 19
June 21 – Carthage, Missouri, to Galena, Kansas, to Vinita, Oklahoma
84 miles (total miles – 1,062)
Sunny, 95 degrees, with a headwind

Tracy
    We get up early and are on the road by 6:30 a.m. to try to beat the heat. Twenty-four miles into the ride, we cross into Kansas, our fourth state. There are only thirteen miles of Route 66 in Kansas. We bicycle through three communities, one being the city of Galena, which has totally embraced the Route 66 theme.

The 1.2-mile section of road from the Missouri state line to Galena is listed on the National Register of Historic Places as the Kansas Route 66 Historic District—East Galena. The city is also known for The Cars on the Route Café. The café is a former Kan-O-Tex Service Station that has been turned into a deli. The other cool thing about the deli is the "Tow Mater" tow truck. This early 1950s International Harvester truck was made famous in the Disney movie *Cars* (2006). Sir Tow Mater is parked on the street in front of the deli and draws a lot of attention. We have not seen the movie yet, but I guess we have to now.

Peter

Six miles west of Galena, or two miles west of Riverton, is the Rainbow Bridge over Bush Creek. Built in 1923, this is the only remaining single-span concrete Marsh arch bridge on the entire length of Route 66.

The bridge is on a narrow one-way road which runs parallel to the new road, so it should be a relaxing transit. However, as we start to cross the bridge, we almost run into a woman from a group of tourists who is taking pictures in the middle of the road. She has her back to us and is right in our path. I slow us down to a crawl, move over to the left, and call out, "Passing on your left. Passing on your left." When she finally hears me, she almost backs right into us. It's a good thing I was paying attention.

Ten miles further, and just south of Baxter Springs, we enter the great state of Oklahoma. Thirteen miles more and we arrive in the city of Commerce, the boyhood home of baseball great Mickey Mantle (1931-1995). It is funny because as we are bicycling through town, Tracy sees a baseball field and comments, "That is an amazing field. It must be something special." At the time we did not know Commerce is the boyhood home of Mr. Mantle and that the beautiful field was built in his honor. Too funny!

The Rainbow Bridge over Bush Creek, just west of Galena, Kansas, is the only remaining single-span concrete Marsh arch bridge on Route 66. You can still see the inattentive tourists who nearly backed into us behind Peter.

The next town is Miami, where we bicycle right by the Coleman Theater. Built in 1929 in the Spanish Mission Style, it is quite an impressive building. Back in the day, the theater was part of the Orpheum Vaudeville circuit and hosted the likes of the Three Stooges, Tom Mix, and Will Rogers.

Our route today is primarily along Route 66, which crosses Interstate 44, or the Will Rogers Turnpike, several times. Will Rogers (1875-1935) was a vaudeville performer, actor, humorous social commentator, and "Oklahoma's Favorite Son." The turnpike opened to traffic in 1957 and was designated I-44 in 1958.

Tracy

The last thirty miles to Vinita (pop. 5,453) are tough! It is getting hotter, windier, and a bit hillier. We are glad to get into our hotel room and cool down. After more than 1,000 miles of riding, we are starting to wonder why we are carrying our camping gear; we have not camped once since our trip began.

Peter

Not camping while bicycle touring is strange for us. We both love to camp, and it is usually our first choice for lodging. Our seven-foot, six-inch by four-foot, six-inch, five-pound, twelve-ounce REI Half Dome tent is like our home away from home. Everything has its place and we are quite comfortable there. Frankly we miss it. Normally, we split our nights evenly between camping, hotels and Warmshowers stays on tours. This pattern has held true during the past two years and over 7,000 miles of self-supported bicycle travel across the United States in all kinds of environments and weather.

There are advantages and disadvantages to all three types of lodging. Camping is our favorite and usually cost-effective (although campsites were going for $70 per night in Maine in the summer of 2014 during our Northern Tier trip). However, sometimes we cannot find a campground, or lately, it is so hot that it would be hard to sleep if we camped, and we need our sleep. Sleeping during thunderstorms or when Tracy thinks there are bear about (See our book *Coast to Coast on a Tandem*) can be difficult as well.

Warmshowers stays are nice, free, and the companionship can be just what the doctor ordered on a long, lonely tour, but we cannot always find hosts, particularly in sparsely populated areas. Plus, sometimes we just need our own space. Hotels are usually okay, but sometimes they are fully booked, very expensive, or nonexistent. At this point, our tent and other camping gear are just dead weight, but we are still glad to have them.

This sign confirmed we were on the right track as we made our way through some warm rides in Oklahoma.

Chapter 5

State of Oklahoma

June 22-27, 2016
432 miles/1,417 total

Day 20
June 22 – Vinita to Tulsa, Oklahoma
67 miles (total miles – 1,129)
Sunny, 95 degrees, with a headwind

Tracy

This morning, I decide to make sure our tracker is still working. I pull up the website on our computer and there is our dot, right in our hotel room in Vinita, Oklahoma. It is kind of creepy, but at the same time nice for friends and family following us, and in case of an emergency.

Our ride generally follows Route 66 today, which makes navigating easy

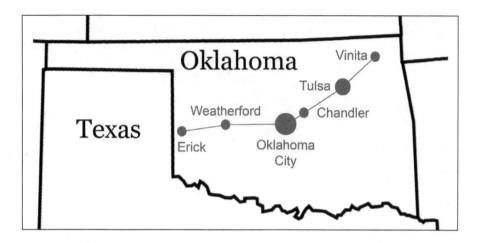

for me. We travel through many small towns, several without services, so we do not stop.

Three miles west of the twin bridges over the Verdigris River and one mile east of the city of Catoosa, we see the famous Blue Whale of Catoosa. The whale is eighty feet long by twenty feet tall and sits on the edge of a spring-fed pond. It was constructed in 1972 by Hugh S. Davis, using concrete sides and a steel frame. Visitors used to love swimming in the pond and diving off the whale's tail. Even though you cannot swim in the pond anymore, visitors are still allowed to explore the whale. You can walk through its mouth all the way back to its tail. It definitely is a Route 66 must see. We decided not to stop because of the heat, headwind, and because we can't cool off in the pond. Bummer!

Slightly further down the road, we see the Tulsa skyline and are excited to get to the city to check it out. Our plans are to take a day off in Tulsa (pop. 404,086), and our Warmshowers host has graciously agreed to put us up for two nights. We head directly to our host's house to get out of the incessant heat.

Robyn's home is surrounded by fabulous gardens. As we chat briefly outside, we learn that Robyn is a Master Gardener. Her gardens are a tribute to her knowledge and expertise. Inside the house (and in the blessed air conditioning), we meet Robyn's boyfriend, Mike, and all of their animals. There is Mike's dog, Sandy; Robyn's foster failure standard poodle, Maya; her toy poodle, Sammy; and Cootie, the cat. Maya, apparently, loves to sneak in their guests' room and steal a toothbrush or bicycle glove. Not to chew, but just to carry out into the yard. It doesn't take long for Maya to welcome us in her own special way. Robyn suggests we should keep our door closed.

After we get cleaned up, Robyn and Mike take us downtown for a neighborhood celebration and dinner at one of their favorite restaurants. We have a fun evening exploring the city. We visit several interesting places, including the Center of the Universe. This is a unique outdoor space, marked by a small concrete circle, with a mysterious acoustic phenomenon. If you stand in the circle and talk, the amplified sound echoes back to you, and you sound distorted to people outside the circle. It is truly amazing. Robyn explains that the city has asked several experts to check out the area to try and determine why it echoes, but no one has yet been able to figure it out.

We head back to our home for the next two days and spend the rest of the evening getting to know each other better. Robyn is an associate professor of biology at Tulsa Community College, which helps explain the gardens and animals.

Peter is in his glory this evening. Not only are we taking tomorrow off, but he also found Robyn's massage chair. I am not sure I will be able to get him out of it. All too soon, we need to head to bed. I am thrilled we can sleep in tomorrow.

Day 21
June 23 – Tulsa, Oklahoma
0 miles (total miles – 1,129)
Sunny, very hot, 97 degrees

Peter

We are so glad to be off the bike today with wonderful Warmshowers hosts in Tulsa. We sleep in and take our time getting up. Breakfast consists of scrambled fresh eggs from the chicken coop in the back yard, fresh fruit, coffee, and sausage. So good.

It is even hotter today than yesterday, so Mike offers to take us by car to run some errands. We go to the post office to mail souvenirs, maps, and receipts home, and I get a much-needed haircut. I want my hair as short as possible because of the heat, but not so short that my head gets sunburned through the air vents in my helmet.

Later in the day, we go out with Robyn. I drive her Toyota Prius because she is recovering from eye surgery. It feels strange to be driving a car again after twenty-one days on the bike, but the familiarity of the Prius helps. We pick up some chain lube at a bike shop, get a snack at a local coffee shop, and tour more of Tulsa. When we return home, we even get a tour of the storm shelter in Robyn's garage. Storm shelters are very common in Oklahoma because of the high tornado risk. Robyn and her animals have spent many hours huddled in the shelter. Fortunately, they have never been hit by a tornado. (The top three states for tornadoes (1997-2022) were Texas, Kansas, and Oklahoma. May, April, and June are the most active months for tornadoes.) Fingers crossed, we still have a lot of Oklahoma to cover, and Texas is up next. It is fun to see Tulsa along with two people who know it so well.

We order in for dinner and spend a relaxing evening watching TV and talking about Robyn's passions of biking and rafting. I finish off the evening with one last chair massage.

The kindness of complete strangers, who sometimes become lifelong friends, continues to overwhelm us. Robyn even reached out to a friend in Albuquerque, New Mexico, to let him know we are coming his way.

Thank you, Robyn and Mike, for being so kind and getting us back on our feet for the next leg of our journey.

Day 22
June 24 – Tulsa to Chandler, Oklahoma
74 miles (total miles – 1,203)
Cloudy, 88 degrees, with a slight head and crosswind

Peter

We are up at 5 a.m. and leave our Warmshowers host's home by 6 a.m. The early start helps us beat the heat and rush hour traffic. Tulsa is a nice city, but its roads are not particularly conducive to bicycle travel. The roads are busy, narrow, and the speed limits do not seem to apply. We thought it wise to get going while the getting was good.

Robyn and Mike have been wonderful hosts, and Robyn and the animals even get up to see us off. Robyn provides us with great directions to get back on route from her house, and before we know it we are out of the city and on our way west again.

(We have kept in touch with Robyn and finally had a chance to see her again in 2022 in Tulsa during a trip to Texas to visit our daughter, Alex. Robyn is retired now and enjoying her newfound freedom. We hope she will come and visit us at our home in Green Bay someday so we can begin to repay her kindness. Buying her a glass of beer and a big pretzel just did not seem like quite enough.)

Touring bicyclists often talk about "karma debt" and the strong need to repay the kindness shown to them, usually by complete strangers. It is a debt most of us will never be able to repay, particularly to those who extend the kindness. Our only real option is to pay the kindness forward. One way we do this is by hosting fellow cyclists in our home whenever we can. Our guest room is called "the bicycle room." Another way is by looking for the opportunity to practice random acts of kindness like those that have been bestowed upon us.

Tracy

We return to Route 66 as we leave Tulsa, and travel through a small town every ten to fifteen miles.

Our 11 a.m. lunch stop is at the historic and famous Rock Café in Stroud, sixty miles into our ride. This 1939 café was placed on the National Register of Historic Places in 2001. The owners also successfully secured a cost share grant from the National Park Service's Route 66 Corridor Preservation Program the same year. They used the grant funds for a top-to-bottom rehabilitation of the café, including returning the dining room to an earlier era with the layout restored to the original floor plan. They also restored the exterior Giraffe-style sandstone. The sandstone was left over from a construction project on Route 66, purchased for $5.00.

We are looking forward to some real food after snacking on the bike all morning. The food is amazing, and Peter absolutely loves his no bun buffalo burger served with sauerkraut. The burger consists of a 1/3-pound organic bison burger patty on top of a bed of greens and pickles, covered with sautéed mushrooms and onions, and topped with parmesan cheese. Peter comments to the waitress how much he enjoyed the sandwich and that he especially liked the parmesan cheese on it. After some discussion and checking with the cook, it is determined the cheese is BelGioioso Cheese, produced in Wisconsin and headquartered on Main Street

The Rock Café in Stroud, Oklahoma, is a historic stop on Route 66.

in Green Bay, maybe seven miles from our house. The waitress says it is the best cheese, and it makes the sandwich.

Peter

BelGioioso Cheese is near and dear to our hearts for a couple of reasons. First, our daughter Melissa's boyfriend (and now husband), Dillon, paid off his college and police academy debts by working long hours at the Denmark, Wisconsin, plant. The work was cold, damp, and hard, but it paid well. The best part of the job for the rest of us, though, was that Dillon got incredible discounts on some of the best cheese in the world. We tried to get him to keep his job at the plant, but he opted for an easier life and became a cop. (I'm kidding, of course.)

Our second connection to the company is that BelGioioso President and founder Errico Auricchio is a bicyclist, and we have done group rides together from time to time. He is a great guy and a good rider, not to mention he makes incredible cheese, including the variety used exclusively on the no bun buffalo burgers at the historic Rock Café in Stroud, Oklahoma.

Tracy

The Rock Café is also famous for the part it plays in the Pixar movie *Cars* (2006). The producers based the character Sally Carrera on the Rock Café's owner, Dawn Welch. I guess we really do have to see the movie. Unfortunately, we never did see Dawn.

There is a Route 66-themed gift shop next to the café which we peruse, but do not buy anything. It still feels too early to start stocking up. Besides, souvenirs are tricky on a bicycle tour, they take up room and add weight to our gear. Beer glasses, however, seem to be the exception.

We are starting to see vineyards along the road, and the Stable Ridge Vineyards west of Stroud is supposed to be a good one. Not being wine drinkers, we bypass the winery. One of these days we will have to stop and buy some wine to send home to our daughter, Melissa.

We make it to Chandler (pop. 3,095), our home for the night, early and decide to visit the Route 66 Interpretative Center. The museum is located in a refurbished 1936 armory building. We enjoy a tour with interpretive displays and some beautiful photographs from along the route, and then watch several videos. The viewing areas are a neat design where you sit in the seats of classic cars and even lay on the bed of a makeshift hotel room to watch the video. What a unique way to present the history of Route 66. It is a fun stop, even if we both slept through part of one of the videos. I guess you cannot offer a bed to tired bicyclists to watch a video. It happens!

Peter

We have dinner at B's Restaurant next to our Econo Lodge motel ($54) and call it a day after posting to social media and watching *Blue Bloods* on TV.

Tomorrow, we ride to Oklahoma City, just fifty-two miles away.

Day 23
June 25 – Chandler to Oklahoma City, Oklahoma
52 miles (total miles – 1,255)
Sunny, 94 degrees, with a nasty crosswind at 15 mph from the south

Tracy

It is in the 70s with calm winds when we climb onto the bike this morning. Nice!

Peter

Only one mile south of our motel, we stop briefly to take a picture of an old Phillips 66 filling station. I am reluctant to stop so soon because our stiff muscles are not warmed up yet. We are not in the rhythm of the ride, and I want to get some miles under our belt before we take a break. But this beautiful little green building is calling to me. According to a nearby sign, this 1930 station is typical of the type "B" cottage-style built by Phillips Petroleum 1927 through 1938. These relics are an unofficial symbol of Route 66 and a must stop. http://route66times.com/l/ok/chandler-phillips-66-station.htm

Tracy

The first community we come to today that embraces the Route 66 spirit is the small town of Arcadia (pop. 199) about thirty miles into the ride. We bicycle right by "Bubbles," a 66-foot-tall soda bottle sculpture and the accompanying soda-centered roadhouse named "Pops," which debuted on Route 66 in 1972. Bubbles is made from stacked steel hoops with thousands of color-shifting LEDs. It evidently is the world's largest soda bottle. The Arcadia Round Barn is the other attraction we are excited to see.

Peter

The Arcadia Round Barn along historic Route 66 is both a landmark and a tourist attraction. The barn was built by local farmer William Harrison Odor in 1898. It measures sixty feet in diameter, forty-three feet tall, and is made of native bur oak. Oak boards were soaked while green and formed into curves for the walls and roof rafters. The barn's magnificent loft was built to hold hay, but also for dances, weddings, and other special events. The circular construction of the barn was believed to make the structure "cyclone-proof" in the early twentieth century. While there is no scientific evidence to this effect, so far, so good.

Tracy

The barn was rapidly deteriorating when it was placed on the National Register of Historic Places in 1977, and it was severely dilapidated by May of 1988 when the Arcadia Historical and Preservation Society was formed. In fact, the barn's condition was so bad that the decaying roof completely collapsed in June of that year. Undaunted, a group of volunteers got together

The Arcadia Round Barn was built by a local farmer in 1898. Volunteers renovated the structure and the City of Arcadia now owns the building.

to save the barn, and it is now owned by the city.

It is great to see what volunteers can do when they all pull in the same direction. While we are touring the barn, two gentlemen are touching up the paint on it, and it looks great.

All too soon, our visit is over and we climb back onto the bicycle for the last twenty miles to Oklahoma City. We were told that this part of Oklahoma was pretty much flat. NOT. There are many long, gentle hills; the kind that wear out your legs as you climb up one, down the next, and repeat.

The nice, wide shoulder we have been enjoying the past couple of days is nowhere to be found as we continue west, mainly on Route 66. Peter is struggling today and complaining about being hot, that the predicted crosswind has just enough gusty headwind to make it a pain, the road is only two lanes, narrow with no shoulder, everyone and their brother seems to be driving Route 66 today, and he just cannot get his legs to produce much power. (Translation: Peter is grumpy!)

Peter

Next up is Oklahoma City (pop. 640,010). Like all big cities, Oklahoma City stretches on and on. First, we hit the outer ring suburbs with a bit of a rural feel. Then, the roads get wider and the traffic gets heavier. We stop for a snack and coffee at Starbucks in Edmond. Hopped up on caffeine and sugar, we then make our final push to OKC. Fortunately, today is a Saturday and the traffic is manageable. Our route does take us through some quiet, very elite, old neighborhoods that we learned later were built with oil money. Tomorrow morning (Sunday), heading out of town early should be a breeze.

We are spending the night only a couple of miles off route at a Holiday Inn

Express. Tracy had put out feelers to four Warmshowers hosts over the past few days, but no luck. They are probably all out bicycling.

Once we get cleaned up, we take an Uber to Belle Isle Restaurant & Brewery, only a few miles away. Both the dinner and the beer are good. The only funny thing for us is that all they serve is 3.2 beer. Apparently, by law, this low-alcohol variety is all they can make since they serve food. We sure hope real beer tastes okay in the souvenir glass we bought.

A history lesson in 3.2 beer

Three-two beer, light beer, 3.2 beer, or low-point beer, were popular terms in the 1930s. They described beers that contain 3.2 percent alcohol by weight (ABW) or 4 percent alcohol by volume (ABV).

Following the end of prohibition in 1933 with the passage of the Twenty-first Amendment, which repealed the Eighteenth Amendment of 1919, some "dry" states continued to ban the production and sale of alcohol. However, with the passage of time, even these states began to loosen their restrictions. The number 3.2 became a rallying point for change. The number 3.2 came from Anton J. Carlson, the Physiology Department chairperson at the University of Chicago. Carlson deemed 3.2 percent ABW as the standard for non-intoxication. In other words, he determined a person could still walk (or ride) a straight line after drinking 3.2 beer.

Peter

In looking at our maps after dinner, we discover that we had been climbing all day and we will be for many days to come. Hopefully, that had something to do with why I was having an off/ grumpy day. Tomorrow morning, we hope to visit the Outdoor Symbolic Memorial to the victims of the 1995 bombing of the Alfred P. Murrah Federal Building on our way out of town.

Day 24
June 26 – Oklahoma City to Weatherford, Oklahoma
76 miles (total miles – 1,331)
Warm, 89 degrees, partly cloudy with a strong cross and headwind

Peter

Reluctantly, we decide not to visit the Oklahoma City bombing memorial this morning. The memorial is five miles south of our planned route, and we do not think we have the energy or time to make the detour, especially with the expected heat and headwind. This is one more site we will add to our "We need to get back here someday" list.

The ride west out of the city is uneventful. Although the roads are still large, there is almost no traffic to contend with on this quiet Sunday morning. We are near the town of Bethany, about eight miles into the ride, and cruising right along. Then suddenly, BANG!

"What the hell was that?" I yell to Tracy.

"The rear tire blew," she yells back.

Sitting almost directly on top of the rear wheel on the back of the tandem, Tracy has a "front row seat" to the explosion.

"Were good," I reply.

Fortunately, the front tire is the one that controls most of our steering so I still have plenty of control, although the bike is a bit wobbly. I ease the bike to the side of the road and stop safely.

We drag the bike onto the lawn in front of Southern Nazarene University's (est. 1899) Broadhurst Physical Education Center. In a highly synchronized set of movements, honed over years of practice, we begin to repair the tire. First, I hold the bike while Tracy removes the tent and rear panniers. Next, we switch positions and Tracy holds the rear of the bike while I release the rear rim brake to create space for the tire. Tracy then lifts the back of the bike and I unscrew and remove the rear axle skewer that holds the wheel in place, derail the disgustingly dirty chain from the cogs, and remove the wheel. Only now does Tracy lay the bike gently onto the grass. No words have been spoken between us; we do not need them.

"Why are flats always the rear tire?" I laugh.

While I inspect the tire, Tracy removes the mini bicycle pump from the frame and the bright-red emergency repair kit bag (formerly a stuff sack for a down vest a girlfriend's mother made me in high school) from an outside pocket on one of the large panniers. She retrieves a spare innertube from the bag, partially inflates it with the minipump to speed my tire change, and then sets it within my reach on the grass. Upon inspection, I discover that the rear tire blew with such force that it tore a hole in the sidewall of the tire and put a two-inch hole in the inner tube. Both the tire and the tube are now trash. We have everything we need to fix the rear wheel, including a spare tire, and get it taken care of fairly quickly. I wipe my filthy hands on my bike shorts (that's one of the reasons they are black, you know) and we're back on the road again.

Three miles down the road, we come to Lake Overholser and Tracy tells me to turn left onto a very nice bicycle path to continue west. Left was correct, but not onto the bicycle path. We end up traveling along the east side of the lake instead of across the north end. By the time we figure things out, we are almost two miles off route. Oops, it happens. Finally reoriented, we turn around and head back north to get back on route. On a good note, the lake is beautiful and we are now very familiar with the bicycle trail. We still have about forty-five miles to go to Weatherford and the temperature is almost 90 degrees. I am glad we played it safe this morning and did not try and visit the memorial in Oklahoma City.

Tracy

We are finally back on route, my bad, and are traveling on a section of original Route 66, which is located just north of I-40. Riding so close to the

Nothing like a blown rear tire to start the day. Fortunately, this is not our first rodeo.

interstate has its advantages as gas stations, restaurants, hotels, etc., are only a short detour away. The traffic noise and view of the lovely freeway are definite disadvantages.

Weary, and with about twenty miles to go, we begin to look for a place to take a break, and what do our wandering eyes see, but a Love's Travel Stop sign. With happy hearts, we detour to the Love's located at the intersection of Highway 281 and I-40, just east of the small town of Bridgeport (pop. 113). We know snacks, drinks, and air conditioning await. We have also learned Love's sells cups of fresh fruit on ice. The watermelon is especially refreshing, and Peter and I each devour a cup quickly. Yummy.

Fueled up, we continue west. We see an interesting building near the town of Hydro and decide to take a short break to check it out. A historical marker tells us about the service station which opened in 1927 and was purchased by Lucille and Carl Hamons in 1941. Lucille, known as the "Mother of the Mother Road," operated the gas station (now with a restaurant) until she passed away in 2000. While the original building is now closed, it is a good place to take a break and learn some local history. The building was placed on the National Register of Historic places in 1998. There is a replica of the original building in Weatherford, our ending spot for the day. We will have to check that out as well.

Peter

The rest of the ride is uneventful, with one exception. While we are waiting at a traffic light at a large intersection to turn left from the left turn lane, a truck pulling a trailer with an ATV on it passes us on our right. As the truck moves through the intersection, we watch in amazement as the trailer detaches from the truck and continues straight down the road all by itself.

We are expecting the trailer to flip and crash spectacularly at any moment, but nope, the trailer gently slows and pulls to the left shoulder of the road. It was almost as if someone was driving the trailer. The guy behind the wheel of the truck eventually realizes the trailer is missing, pulls to the right shoulder, and stops. We see him get out of the truck and look around. When he spots the trailer, he puts the truck in reverse and backs across four lanes of traffic to the trailer. The driver gets out of the truck, hooks up the trailer and drives off, almost like this happens all the time. Very strange. This could have been very bad, but no harm, no foul, I guess.

We arrive safely in Weatherford about 5 p.m. It has been a long, but adventurous day on the bicycle.

Tracy

We walk to Lucille's Roadhouse Diner, which is right next door to our hotel, for dinner. This is the replica of the one we stopped at in Hydro. The diner looks like the original and the historic treasures displayed are amazing. We even find a caricature of Lucille near a picture of the original building. The food is delicious.

Facebook follower

Darlene Luedtke Charles (Bellin Health Fitness Center, Green Bay)
June 26, 2016

Hi guys! I happened to think of you both as I'm sitting here on my comfortable lazy boy watching a PBS show on biking. Not sure what it's called; my husband just changed the channel, Grrr .... anyway the TV show reminded me of the two of you bikers. Enjoy, Enjoy, Enjoy your time together.

Day 25
June 27 – Weatherford to Erick, Oklahoma
86 miles (total miles – 1,417)
Partly sunny, 85 degrees, tailwind in morning, crosswind in afternoon

Peter

There were storms last night, and we were glad to be in our hotel room. According to the radar, there is still some rain between us and Clinton, twenty miles to the west, but it is clearing. The weather forecast calls for slightly cooler temperatures and a tailwind, at least in the morning.

We roll out at sunrise to take full advantage of the cool, easterly breeze. The only catch is that as the sun began to rise, the sky looks a bit ominous to the north and east. Heading west, the roads are a bit damp and it is cloudy, but thankfully there is no rain. A slight tailwind has materialized as promised. We are still climbing overall, and there are a lot of ups and downs, and more ups, so we cannot take full advantage of the tailwind. We make good time and by 11 a.m. we are halfway done. The only problem is that we still

The National Route 66 Museum in Elk City, Oklahoma, features a sign you can't miss.

have halfway to go and the wind has now switched to a headwind. With no other choice, we put our heads down and grind it out.

Tracy

The National Route 66 Museum is located in Elk City, a little over forty miles into our ride. We stop for a picture, but do not go in. The museum is listed as a must see in some of the Route 66 literature and probably would be fun to explore, but we just can't. This is one of the hard things about bicycle touring: sometimes you just do not have the time to check out something or it is off route a bit and you don't have the energy for the detour. Oh well, I guess this is one more site we will add to our "We need to get back here someday" list.

A young man is admiring the bike at one of our many gas station/convenience store stops when I return to the bicycle with full water bottles. He asks me about our trip and how it is going. He said he would love to bicycle across the country someday, and then goes on to explain that he had walked Route 66 last year. He told me it took him five months and he really enjoyed the adventure. Upon heading back inside, I notice he has a big backpack on with his tennis shoes dangling from it. I plan to ask him where he is off to this time, but when I come back out, he is gone.

Ah, the glamorous life of a Route 66 bicycling trip.

Facebook follower

Darlene Luedtke Charles
My husband and I took Route 66 on our honeymoon nearly 44 years ago, in a '53 Ford, which he had restored. That is one thing on my bucket list, maybe on our 45th wedding anniversary. Problem is we no longer have the '53 Ford.

We are traveling through the prairie/grassland areas in Oklahoma today. It is really pretty with large expanses of grassland and hills. The towns we encounter are small and spread out. We have enjoyed Oklahoma and will be sad to leave it tomorrow. The people here are very kind and welcoming.

Peter
We make it to Erick (pop. 1,029) by 4 p.m. Never heard of it, I'm not surprised. They have a Days Inn, a Love's Travel Stop with a Subway, and a Simple Simon's Pizza joint (not bad).

Tracy
We are standing outside the Love's in Erick when an older woman approaches us. She asks about our trip and wants to know all the details. She then welcomes us to her town and says how great it is that we are here. She apologizes that their museum is closed and we will not be able to see it unless we stay in town until Tuesday. We explain we really need to continue on our way. She is so genuine about everything that we truly feel welcomed to the town of Erick!

Peter
The highlight of the day was when I rescued a turtle from the middle of the road. (Not a sea turtle, Alex Flucke, but it will have to do.) The lowlight was doing our laundry by hand in the motel room sink, first time this trip though.

We are doing well and having fun, but this is a lot of work and I am starting to get sunburned on my left arm, the one that faces south all day. We are really looking forward to taking another day off the bike in Amarillo, Texas, in three days!

Facebook conversation

WE BIKE, etc.
June 27, 2016 · Erick, Oklahoma
Well, after 1,400 miles of bicycling, and even with applying SPF 50 sunscreen religiously every two hours, Peter finally got too much sun on his arms. Any suggestions BayCare Clinic, LLP or anyone else? **26 Comments**

Bob Carter (Chad Carter's dad)
Wear long sleeves.

Peter Flucke
Bob, I know, but it's really hot here. Lol

Mike Gerke (Friend, pedicab entrepreneur, Ironman)
Long sleeves / arm coolers. Many ultra-runners are wearing long white pants and shirts. Check out Badwater ultra for testimony.

Michelle Bachaus
I wore an unbuttoned sun shirt during peak hours in Australia, but cold/wet rag immediately then many layers of pure aloe - always better by the morning.

Allan Dunlop (International bicycle educator)
Aloe vera (the real thing direct from the plant, not a mix in a lotion) has worked well for me in this situation. Placebo effect? I'm not sure, but it seemed to me to work. (My background is in science and I can tend to be a skeptic, so I don't toss out suggestions lightly.)

Ann Evans Dettlaff
Yep, what they said, aloe and cool packs for some relief.

Cleva Bickford (Doug Instenes's mother-in-law)
Rinse skin with white vinegar.

Darlene Luedtke Charles
Ouch! Back in the day they called that a farmer's tan...

Anne Duggan
My sister swears by sleeves made to wick off the sweat and protect her skin. Bought it at REI, I think.

Anne Duggan
Also, we did a weekend ride along the Mississippi last weekend. There was no way to keep even SPF 50 sunscreen on to protect from burns. It was brutal!

Allan Dunlop
In five years or so of teaching learn-to-ride and other cycling courses in Austin, TX (sometimes for 8 hours in temps of 100 F), much of the time I wore hiking pants and long-sleeved wicking shirts. The hydration pack I packed with ice cubes before putting the water in helped.

John Trester (Member, Bay Shore Bicycle Club, Green Bay)
Burn, burn, burn, that ring of fire...

John Z. Wetmore (*Perils for Pedestrians* producer)
Rub with ice cubes.

Jennifer Klaus (Neighbor)
Tracy can hold an umbrella.

Peter Flucke
Best answer yet Jennifer!

Barb Erb
Jojoba oil...similar to our natural skin oil, it soaks in and revives burnt skin. Look in a natural foods store.

Peter Flucke
Do you think the Love's truck stop across the road carries it?

Dale Nimmo (Warmshowers host in Springfield, Missouri)
Any natural foods store has it.

Laura Andrews (Peter's college friend and outdoors woman extraordinaire)
Being the uber burning redhead I am, long sleeve sun resistant clothing, with lots and lots of vents?

Peter's sunburned arms were beginning to match his shirt by the time we got to Erick, Oklahoma.

Peter Flucke
Rode all day in my long sleeve Columbia camping shirt. Wicks well so I stayed relatively cool, and best of all, I didn't get any sun on my arms. Thanks for the suggestions everyone, I'm good!

Laura Andrews
If it wicks I'd suggest wearing until the burn is cleared up and if you begin to overheat, douse yourself with water.

Brenda Peotter (Bellin Health Fitness Center, Green Bay)
Nice selfie Peter! lol

John Trester
Sunbrella fabric.

The panoramic views in Texas allowed us to see and the winds to build for miles.

Chapter 6

State of Texas

June 28-July 1, 2016
181 miles/1,598 total

Day 26
June 28 – Erick, Oklahoma, to Groom, Texas
77 miles (total miles – 1,494)
Warm, 87-94 degrees, sunny, slight cross and tailwind

Peter

The first part of our ride to Texola, Oklahoma (pop. 36), just east of the Texas border, is relatively flat. It is cool (low 70s), and the wind is calm.

Tracy

About ten miles into our ride, we enter the Lone Star State. It is really beautiful here, although we are climbing again. The views are amazing through the open grassland.

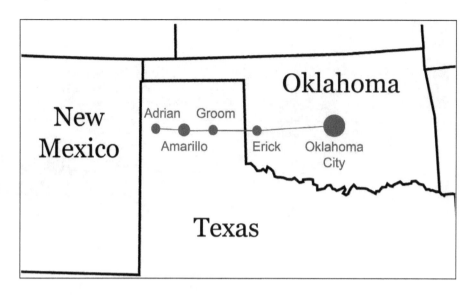

Peter

We start to climb, and climb, and climb once we enter Texas! We are going so slowly at some points that it almost feels like our tires are flat. Then, of course, good OLD Route 66 starts to deteriorate. Much of the road is concrete and many of the joints are starting to fail. We are forced to move from one side of the road to another to avoid flatting a tire in the worst of the potholes and gaps. This is hard to do going uphill, because the weight of the tandem is difficult to control at slow speeds. What is worse, though, is going downhill fast. The bumps and holes in the road come up so quickly that they are almost impossible to avoid without slowing. So slow we do. With precious little downhill, it seems unfair that we can't just let the bike roll.

A few miles outside of Shamrock, I decide that the front and rear tires are not handling the bumps the same. To avoid a possible flat, we pull over to check the tire pressure. The front tire is spot on, 115 psi. The rear tire, on the other hand, is at 60 psi. Seriously! We just climbed 1,000 feet in elevation on a half-inflated tire. No wonder the climb seemed so bad. I top off the tire and life gets much better. We have no idea how the pressure got so low. Hopefully, the tire will stay properly inflated for the rest of the day.

Tracy

The first town we come to in Texas is Shamrock, which has one of the most iconic symbols of Route 66, Tower Station and U-Drop Inn Café. It is a beautifully restored art deco building that now is the home of the chamber of commerce and the department of tourism. We, of course, are here before it opens (Tuesday 9 a.m.-5 p.m.), so we cannot tour the inside.

We are happy someone is saving these iconic buildings; many we have seen along the route have not been so lucky. The building, built in 1936, was home to the Tower Conoco Station and U-Drop Inn Café. It was the first commercial business located on the newly designated Route 66 in Shamrock. Today it is considered one of the most iconic and architecturally creative buildings along the length of the road.

Our next stop is the town of McLean, which claims to have the "First Route 66 Museum." Lots of communities have Route 66 museums, but this one claims to be the first. We skip the museum and have a great lunch at a small café/market in town. McLean has a population of about 800 people, yet offers quite a bit for such a small town. They even have the Devil's Rope Museum, where evidently, you can learn everything you ever wanted to know about barbed wire. We skip that museum, too.

Our ride today has just a few small towns. The populations of these towns are between thirty-six and about 2,000, so we really have to plan ahead to make sure we

This Tower Conoco Station and U-Drop Inn Café has been wonderfully restored in Shamrock, Texas.

have enough water and food for the long stretches of open space. We do just fine.

Peter

Just west of Alanreed, our route takes us on the shoulder of I-40 for about six miles. There are no other roads to ride on. We have ridden on interstate highways before in Montana and North Dakota during our Northern Tier trip, so this is nothing new to us. There is a nice, wide, fifteen-foot shoulder to ride on and we are protected by rumble stripes. It is no big deal as long as we use extreme caution at the on and off ramps.

We try to cross at the narrowest point to improve our safety at freeway ramps. The less time we spend in the path of speeding motor vehicles, who are not expecting to encounter bicyclists, the better. We avoid crossing at the beginning of the ramps, where the distance is greatest, and instead ride the shoulder part way down the ramp. When Tracy, who is looking back over her shoulder for overtaking traffic, yells "Clear!" we cut back to the main road shoulder at a ninety-degree angle. If there is no safe gap in traffic, we simply continue down the ramp and then ramp back on the other side.

The fatality rate for a bicyclist struck by a motorist going just 30 mph is approximately 50 percent. At 60 mph, the fatality rate is almost 100 percent. The speed limit on this stretch of interstate is 75 mph.

Tracy

For the first time on this trip, we have to ride on I-40. It sounds scarier than it is. The motor vehicle drivers are great and typically pull over to the left lane when they go by. We especially like the professional truck drivers. They just get it, and when at all possible, move over one lane for us. They also are typically friendly, and it is not uncommon for us to receive a little beep-beep and a wave when they go by.

Peter

One advantage of riding on the interstate is that there are rest areas with water, bathrooms, air conditioning, and snacks. We stop at one for a short break. Several other travelers in the parking lot look at us quizzically as we roll in. Eventually, a couple wander over to ask, "What the heck are you doing here on your bicycle?" We laugh and explain that historic Route 66 takes us on the interstate because there are no other roads available for us to get through the area. This sparks a rush of the usual questions, "Where are you from?" "You bicycled all this way?" "Where are you going?" We have heard them all before and happily answer every last one.

The Gray County Safety Rest Area sits on a high hill and has amazing views. It also has interpretative information inside about the wind turbines, which are abundant in this area.

After exiting the interstate, we have another twenty miles to ride to Groom (pop. 566) our ending point for the day. The road finally levels out five or so miles east of Groom, and we pick up a tailwind. We make it to our motel by 3:30 p.m. It is nice to be in early for a change. We are spending the night at the Chalet Inn. What a pleasant surprise. Even though it is an old property, it is clean and comfortable. Just what a couple of hot and tired bicyclists need.

Groom is known for the Leaning Tower of Texas, a nonworking water tower that was brought in as a marketing ploy. The owner, Roger Britten, bought the tower from an adjacent town and purposefully installed it at an 80-degree angle, with two legs in the ground and two dangling in midair. His truck stop and restaurant were very popular with this attraction. Unfortunately, there is no longer a restaurant or truck stop here, but the Leaning Tower remains and got us to stop and take a look.

Facebook followers

Rebecca Cleveland (Bike shop owner)
So... is everything bigger and better? I have driven through Erick and Groom numerous times... it's like "Groundhogs Day!" Did you see the leaning (water) tower of Groom and the world's largest cross in the western hemisphere? Amazing the stuff you see in the middle of nowhere! Next up, the Cadillac graveyard in Amarillo.

Peter Flucke
We saw the water tower this afternoon and will see the cross, God willing, tomorrow morning on our way out of town. Any suggestions for things to do in Amarillo?

Robyn Stroup (Warmshowers host in Tulsa, Oklahoma)
Quarterhorse Museum. You'd need to rent a car to get to the Palo Duro Canyon, but it's beautiful. Cadillac Ranch on your way west.

Richard C. Moeur (Traffic Engineer, Arizona Department of Transportation)
Obey the Texas Stop Sign. If you ride the bike there, especially on a tandem (right, Suzanne?) the calories don't count. I don't know if Nick Gerlich is following your adventures – I'll tag him in case he's up by Amarillo tomorrow.

Nancy Hart (Peter's high school friend)
Yay! Welcome to my state, Peter.

Peter Flucke
Nan, where do you live?

Nancy Hart
Dallas. 334 miles south and a bit east of you.

Peter Flucke
Maybe we will catch you on our next trip through. Not sure we are up for adding another 668 miles to our trip. Lol

Post from our marketing specialist, Kat:
Have you taken a look at our blog by Tracy Flucke lately? You should! Tracy's perspective on our adventure, from the stoker seat of the tandem, is unique. This is also where we post many of the GoPro videos she shoots throughout the day. Enjoy!

For dinner, we discover this little ice cream place known locally as DQ. No, really! It is our only choice for food, other than the gas station next door. (And our diets were going so well, too!)

We are excited for tomorrow. We are only forty-seven miles away from Amarillo and will be taking Thursday off.

Day 27
June 29 – Groom to Amarillo, Texas
52 miles (total miles – 1,546)
67 degrees and stormy in morning, hot afternoon, 94 degrees, tailwind

Tracy

We eat a quick breakfast in our hotel room of coffee, tea, instant oatmeal, bananas, and muffins with peanut butter, then we are on the road. The weather is marginal and a storm is coming our way, but after checking the radar and listening to the forecast, we are fairly confident we have enough time to get to Conway, sixteen miles away, before it hits. The terrain is dead flat, and the weather is a pleasant 69 degrees with a light easterly tailwind.

On our way out of Groom, we see the "World's Largest Cross," our friend Rebecca told us about. It is reported to be the biggest cross in the Western Hemisphere at 190 feet tall. The cross is as large as the neighboring wind turbines, so it's hard to miss.

Peter

The wind abruptly shifts to the north (a crosswind) five miles into the ride and increases to 15-25 mph. This is no big deal as the storm clouds are still a comfortable distance to the north, although we are now moving much more slowly. At this point, I start looking for possible shelter, freeway underpasses, grain elevators, etc., just in case.

With a grain elevator, and likely shelter, far off in the distance, we continue west. The clouds are beautiful, but I notice they are starting to form a wall, and they are getting closer. I do not say anything to Tracy, yet I am starting to get concerned. As a trained weather spotter who has seen more than his share of bad weather, including tornadoes, I know this cloud formation could indicate a strong gust front, unrideable and possibly dangerous conditions. Then we start to see rain and finally, LIGHTNING!

Although I used to make high-risk traffic stops and search dark buildings for bad guys with guns as a cop, I do not do lightning. Lightning makes me stupid scared, especially out in the open like this. Time to get the hell off the road. We try to pick up our pace, but now the wind is even stronger. Fortunately, by this time we are within a half mile of what we recognize to be a very large old farm equipment storage building, and the door is open. It is not raining yet as we ride straight to the barn so we can take cover if need be. The radar on my smartphone does not look promising.

Tracy

When we finally get to the pole barn, I really need to go to the bathroom and wander around the back side to find a spot. As our primary navigator, I carry the map safely tucked in a plastic bag (in case of rain) in my back pocket. When I stand up after doing my thing, the map flies out of my pocket and away it goes. $#!+! ... I take off after it, but the wind is so strong there is no way I will catch it. The map blows across a driveway and is heading toward farm fields that stretch as far as the eye can see. The map is gone and will probably end up in New Mexico. Now what? Peter is going to kill me. Miraculously, the plastic bag gets hung up on the barb wire fence surrounding the fields. Thank goodness! I run over, snatch the map and hold it tight to my chest. I am so glad I do not have to tell Peter I lost the map.

Peter

This is not the first time that Tracy has, almost, lost our map out in the middle of nowhere. When we were riding across the country on the Northern Tier route, we stopped on a two-lane, gravel road near the Idaho/Montana border so she could, again, go to the bathroom. A mile or so after we were back underway, I asked Tracy how far it was to our next turn because I was getting concerned that our gravel road should have turned back to pavement already. Her response, "I lost the map!"

"Seriously?" I replied. Fortunately, we were able to turn around and follow our tire tracks right to the spot where the map had fallen onto the road, right where Tracy had rested it on the back of the bike. Lucky there was not any wind that day.

Fifteen minutes later, the storm hits! There is no thunder or lightning, but the wind and rain are intense. Although the building is dark and dirty, it is dry. I pass the time playing with my phone while Tracy leans up against a piece of farm equipment and goes to sleep. Impressive! Usually I am the one who can sleep anywhere and through anything.

About twenty minutes later, the storm has passed. Fifteen or so minutes after that, the roads are mostly dry and there is a great tailwind. Off to Conway we go.

Tracy

We see two interesting things as we continue our ride to Conway. The first is the Slug Bug Ranch, which is a takeoff of the Cadillac Ranch near Amarillo, but with VW Bugs. The second is two giant guns located at the end of a private driveway. The large revolvers are actually grills that someone placed on either side of their driveway facing out to the street. They are kind of creepy, but then we are in Texas.

Peter

Our next stop is The Big Texan Steak Ranch & Brewery on the eastern side of Amarillo. This is the home of the Free 72-ounce Steak. If you can eat

Our visit to the Slug Bug Ranch

"Slug Bug Ranch, also known as Bug Ranch, Bug Farm, and Buggy Farm, was created in 2002. The five wrecked Volkswagen Beetles, buried hood-down in the ground, were the idea of the Crutchfield family, who owned the Longhorn Trading Post and Rattlesnake Ranch next door.

"It began when a huge corporate Travel Plaza was built on the opposite side of the Crutchfields' interstate exit. They figured they could stay in business if they could siphon away traffic with something eye-catching and engaging. Slug Bug Ranch seemed a natural choice: a parody of the popular Cadillac Ranch, 35 miles west. At the time, the Beetle wrecks were painted a pristine bright yellow, and a sign next to them encouraged, 'Sign a Bug.'

"The Crutchfields were right about one thing: Slug Bug Ranch has proved popular as an attraction. Unfortunately, it didn't work as a business plan, and the Trading Post closed only a year after it was built. While its current state (in late 2022) is a testament to vigorous spray-paint attention endured from Route 66 travelers, the property no longer welcomes foot traffic ('trespassers'). Consider this a drive-by, viewable only from the public road."
(https://www.roadsideamerica.com/story/17024)

it all in one hour, it's free. (Even after bicycling over 1,500 miles, we do not consider giving it a try!) This place is like Disney World meets an authentic Texas roadhouse. The food is good, but the beer is mediocre.

Tracy

We have to stop at the Big Texan Ranch & Brewery after seeing their bill-boards for miles and miles. When we are at the restaurant, two gentlemen are trying to get the free 72-ounce steak dinner. The challengers, who must first pay $72 each, sit at a raised table with spotlights on them and a huge count-down timer. It is rather funny to watch, but at the same time gross. Neither guy finishes within the time limit, so no free meal, only indigestion.

Peter

On our way into the restaurant, we spot a white van with not one, but two custom Calfee tandems on the back. What? This is some serious equipment. Then Tracy spots the Race Across America (RAAM) decals on the van. Holy $#!+, Batman!

According to the event's website, the Race Across America (RAAM) is an ultra-distance road cycling race across the United States. This 3,000-mile classic American tradition has been held annually since 1982 when it was called the Great American Bike Race. The race draws riders from around the world who compete as individuals and teams.

Solo racers have twelve days to complete the journey, and relay teams have nine days. Starting in Oceanside, California, the RAAM route, climbs 175,000 feet and crosses twelve states before finishing in Annapolis, Mary-land. During the race, which always travels west to east, riders traverse three major mountain ranges (Sierra, Rocky, and Appalachian), cross four of America's longest rivers (Colorado, Mississippi, Missouri, and Ohio), and the Great Plains. They also pass through iconic American landmarks such as the Mojave and Sonoran deserts, Monument Valley, and Gettysburg.

As we walk around the huge lobby of the restaurant, we spot a couple wearing matching blue shirts. They look fit; could they be the RAAM riders? So we ask. Yup! Jeanne and Michael not only completed the ride, but they did it in just seven days and won their category! They are amazing and it is a pleasure to talk with them.

Fun facts: Their average speed for the ride was approximately 20 mph, and on their fastest descent they hit 71 mph! We are in the midst of tandem royalty. Remember, it will take us about two months to bicycle across the country and they just did it in seven days. Before parting ways, Jeanne and Mike even offer to let us stay at their house in southern California and ride with them at the end of our trip. How fun would that be. We will have to wait and see if it works out.

Tracy

Jeanne and Mike reached out to us the following year to invite us to be part of a tandem relay team (three other tandem teams) they were putting together to compete in RAAM. We were honored they asked, but riding in RAAM is not my idea of fun. I cannot imagine riding our tandem at top speed for six hours and then sitting, and trying to sleep, in the support van for eighteen hours with four other stinky cyclists, and then repeating that cycle for up to eight more days.

Peter

We are staying at a hotel in Amarillo tonight and tomorrow to rest and recover. Tracy plans to sleep until noon. Having just met the RAAM riders, we must admit to feeling a bit soft.

Day 28
June 30 – Amarillo, Texas
0 miles (total miles – 1,546)

Peter

As usual, I am up before Tracy, but this time I do not wake her to pack, eat breakfast, and get on the bike. It is a day off and I let her sleep.

After a relaxing breakfast at our hotel, we package up some souvenirs to mail home, call an Uber, and head to the Amarillo Botanical Gardens. The gardens are beautiful, and it is fun to see all the different plants and trees that we do not have in Wisconsin. It is also nice to now be able to identify some of the vegetation we are seeing as we roll along.

Facebook followers

Mark Stephany (Green Bay bicyclist and gift card provider – see *Coast to Coast on a Tandem*)
How interesting to meet that RAAM couple!

Cathy Skott
Cool day! Nice meet up!

Dawn N Hal Goodman
You two have the most interesting encounters!

Peter Flucke
True, but I think it's just the law of probabilities. The more you get out, the more encounters you have.

Matt Trahan (Louisiana State Trooper, bicycle racer, Peter's former student)
Great write up and pictures! Cool that y'all met up with them, but no steak? Ha ha. Safe rides!

Peter Flucke
Dude, can you imagine trying to ride the next day after eating that?!

Tracy

We return to the hotel, then go out to lunch, get Peter's regular glasses straightened (riding in the top of his bike pannier has been tough on them), and do a phone interview with Cassandra Duvall of NBC26 in Green Bay, Wisconsin, about our trip. Then we take a nap.

Peter

Well rested, we lay out our tentative schedule for the next several days:

> July 1 (Fri.), Adrian, TX (50 miles)
> July 2 (Sat.), Tucumcari, NM (65)
> July 3 (Sun.), Santa Rosa, NM (60)
> July 4 (Mon.), Las Vegas, NM (71)
> July 5 (Tues.), Santa Fe, NM (64)
> July 6 (Wed.), Albuquerque, NM (75)
> July 7 (Thurs.), Albuquerque, NM (0)

We will be gaining approximately 2,300 feet in elevation to reach 5,800 feet over the next six days. Hopefully, we will find cooler temperatures as we climb.

We do Tex-Mex near our hotel for dinner. Having lived in Honduras when I was a kid, I love beans and rice, and everything that goes with them. Tracy, not so much. She was raised on a typical Midwestern meat and potatoes diet, and this is not that. Sorry, Honey. We are in the land of Tex-Mex. We laugh about the thunderstorm raging outside. We could easily be huddling in our tent right now eating God only knows what. It is only a matter of time.

Day 29
July 1 – Amarillo to Adrian, Texas
52 miles (total miles – 1,598)
Stormy in the morning, warm - 93 degrees, partly sunny,
tailwind after storm went through, then changed to headwind

Peter

Refreshed from our day off the bike in Amarillo, we are ready to ride. The weather report calls for clear skies and a 15-25-mph headwind. Ouch! At least the route is flat today. The hotel breakfast starts at 6:30 a.m. and we are out the door by 7 a.m., only to be met by RAIN! Okay, plan B. Wait 'til it stops. The skies clear after about fifteen minutes and we are on our way.

Our first stop is at a nearby grocery store. We are out of on-bike snacks and need dinner supplies as we are camping tonight, finally.

Tracy

Today is a shorter day for us due to what is available, or not, along the route. We are getting into some more isolated areas again, so we have to plan a bit more to make sure we can get the things we need, like water, food, and shelter.

About five miles into our ride, we once again have to take cover until the rain stops. Luckily, we are on the city of Amarillo's Rock Island Rail Trail and there is a shelter. Waiting out the rain again! After another fifteen-minute delay, we are back at it. The weather is different here. Storms come in very fast and hard, and then a few minutes later they are gone and the sun comes back out. Luckily, we have not been in any real intense storms, just lots of rain and wind. Hopefully, we will not experience a bad storm while we are in Texas.

We see our third Muffler Man just west of Amarillo at the Cadillac RV Park/Cadillac Ranch Gift Store. He's called the Second Amendment Cowboy.

Our next stop is the world-famous Cadillac Ranch. Not sure what to say about this except that someone planted ten Cadillacs in the ground nose-first. Public art? At any rate, people have taken to spray painting the cars and it has become a thing. There are twenty to thirty people here, some painting cars. The best part, though, is that because it had rained, the cars are now in

---

Media coverage

Peter and Tracy Flucke of WE BIKE, etc. will be on NBC26 (Green Bay, WI) Wisconsin tonight at 6:30 (CST) this evening. They will be talking about their tandem bicycle adventure along historic Route 66 from their halfway point in Amarillo, Texas. Check it out!

WE BIKE Route 66 Tour Update

Our WE BIKE partners, Tracy and Peter Flucke, are on the road for their Route 66 bike tour, and have made it over halfway to their Santa Monica, destination. The cycling duo have survived crazy wind and weather, but are loving the trip. Both say their favorite part is meeting new people and learning about all the different places along the way. The couple left on June 3rd, cycling from Green Bay to Chicago, where US Route 66 begins, and plan on staying in Amarillo tonight before beginning the second leg of their trip. In total, Tracy and Peter will be cycling over 2,700 miles, and plan to arrive at Santa Monica Pier on July 20th.

Sarah Grygiel Burdette (Municipal administrator, Tracy's friend)
Glad to see you both are doing well!

Mark Stephany
Thanks for sharing because I did miss it last night. Tracy great job with the daily news!

The famous Cadillac Ranch of Route 66

"Standing along Route 66 west of Amarillo, Texas, Cadillac Ranch was invented and built (1974) by a group of art-hippies imported from San Francisco. They called themselves The Ant Farm, and their silent partner was Amarillo billionaire Stanley Marsh 3. He wanted a piece of public art that would baffle the locals, and the hippies came up with a tribute to the evolution of the Cadillac tail fin. Ten Caddies were driven into one of Stanley Marsh 3's fields, then half-buried, nose-down, in the dirt (supposedly at the same angle as the Great Pyramid of Giza). They faced west in a line, from the 1949 Club Sedan to the 1963 Sedan de Ville, their tail fins held high for all to see on the empty Texas panhandle." (https://www.roadsideamerica.com/story/2220)

a mud pit. People are actually wading into the mud to paint the cars. We stay somewhat mud free, but it is a hoot to watch the other tourists.

Who would think a bunch of cars buried in a field would become so famous and draw people from all over the world? Cadillac Ranch is an iconic must see when traveling historic Route 66.

Peter

Next, we stop at the Hickory Cafe in Vega for lunch. There is not much to Vega (pop. 902), and the cafe looks downright scary from the outside, but there is nowhere else to eat. The fun starts after we go inside and sit down. The only other patron turns out to be a truck driver who regularly drives loads of ... wait for it ... cheese between New Mexico and none other than Green Bay, Wisconsin. You cannot make this stuff up. As we chat with the driver, the cafe starts to fill up. Apparently, this is where all the locals and any stray tourists come to eat. Our food is great, and by the end of the meal, we know maybe half of the folks in the place. We really enjoy our time here.

So far today we have lucked out and been pushed along by a good tailwind. However, now the wind has shifted and we have a 15-mph headwind.

Reaching Adrian, Texas, meant we were officially halfway between Chicago and Los Angeles on Route 66.

No big deal, we only have thirteen more miles to ride to Adrian (pop. 165) and the end of our ride for the day. We take it easy and arrive in Adrian about 2:30 p.m. (temperature 91 degrees).

Tracy

Adrian is the midpoint of Route 66. We know this because the town has painted a thick white line across the four-lane road with the words "Midpoint of Route 66." There is also a large sign along the road welcoming us to Adrian and telling us we are at the midpoint. We are exactly 1,139 miles from Chicago and 1,139 from Los Angeles. In town, we find the Midpoint Café, Midpoint RV Campground, and the Sunflower Station gift shop. We head to the campground first, which is really just ten gravel RV parking pads with hookups. There are no trees, no shade, no one else camping, and crunchy brown grass. Great! Remember, it is 91 degrees.

We are starting to dread the night ahead. Just then, Bud, the campground host, pops out of his trailer to meet us. Bud says, "You could pitch your tent on the grass (in the direct sun) or you can spend the night in the air-conditioned laundry/shower building." Yes please! Bud then tells us to head down to the restaurant because it closes soon, and be sure to stop and talk with Fran at the Sunflower Station. So off we go. We enjoy some delicious pie at the restaurant, featuring what they call "Ugly Crust Pies," and then head next door to Sunflower Station.

Here, we meet Fran Houser and Brodie, her aging Golden Lab. Fran owned the Midpoint Café for many years. She tells us about the history of the café and explains how they discovered that Adrian was the midpoint of Route 66. The café holds the record for being the oldest continuously operating café along U.S. Highway 66 between Amarillo, Texas, and Tucumcari, New Mex-

Our visit with 'Flo' from the movie *Cars*

Fran Houser jokes that her kids say she can talk to a stump. We don't know if that's actually the case, but she certainly does enjoy talking with people. As the owner of Midpoint Café for twenty-four years and later the Sunflower Station gift shop next door, Fran had the opportunity to visit with people from around the world who came through town while experiencing Route 66.

We'll let Fran tell you about some of her more memorable moments during her time owning the café:

"I got to the café one morning and two guys who came in on Harleys were waiting. My waitress didn't show up because of an emergency on her ranch, so I was left to run the grill, take care of the shop, and wait on people by myself. Just then, a busload of Japanese tourists pulled in.

Fran Houser owned the Midpoint Café for many years. She is the person for whom producers of the movie Cars patterned the character Flo, and here she is holding a photo of Flo.

"Before long, a young man stepped into the kitchen and offered to help out. He waited table for about an hour and a half while I worked in the kitchen. After a while, I looked in the dining room and couldn't understand why people were hanging around after they were done eating.

"Someone asked, 'Do you have any idea who's waiting table for you?'

"I said, 'No, but he certainly is appreciated.' It turns out it was actor Bryan Cranston. He was well-known, but I hadn't seen any of his movies and didn't know who he was. I couldn't even take time to go out there and thank him.

"It was kind of slow the day Tracy and Peter showed up. I worried about them because of the eighteen-wheelers on the road, but they did it, and they did it in fine style. It was special to have them with us while they were here."

ico, as well as being the only café on the midpoint between Los Angeles and Chicago.

Besides being a simply delightful woman, Fran is the real-life person for whom they patterned the character Flo in the movie *Cars*. She explains how that occurred and all the fun events she was able to attend because they used her in the film. She gives us a signed copy of a picture of Flo and Flo's V8 Café from the movie. She then asks us to sign the old red Ford pickup truck in front of her shop. It's a Route 66 tradition.

We have not seen the movie *Cars* yet, but plan to try to do that tonight. We carry a small laptop computer to write our blog, do Facebook posts, watch movies, etc. We have spent many a night on other trips enjoying a movie in our small tent. Thanks to my brother Bill, we have Netflix and will see if the movie is available tonight.

Peter

Boy, it is amazing the people you meet when you are on a bicycle. You just never know. As we often say, "On a bicycle, you don't have to look for adventure, adventure finds you!" (Fran no longer owns Sunflower Station, but we have stayed in contact. Sadly, Brodie passed away several years ago.)

Shower, laundry, social media, and bed. No movie, Netflix does not have *Cars*. Darn! On to Tucumcari, New Mexico, tomorrow.

Facebook followers

Darlene Luedtke Charles
I'm lovin' the stories! Keep them coming.

Tracy, I like how your shirt blends with the cars. Almost looks like you planned your wardrobe for this shot.

Noralyn Smiley (Peter's dad's wife)
Sounds like a varied and interesting time, in spite of all the rain. Keep us posted. Always good to know where you are and to hear of your adventures.

We faced a variety of challenges during our trek across the Land of Enchantment.

Chapter 7

State of New Mexico

July 2-July 10, 2016
529 miles/2,127 total

Day 30
July 2 – Adrian, Texas, to Tucumcari, New Mexico
65 miles (total miles – 1,663)
Hot, 92 degrees, windy with 15-mph headwind, partly sunny

Peter

We are up before the sun and plan to be on the road at daybreak again today. We want to have as much flexibility as possible due to the climbing, 15-mph headwinds, temperatures in the lower 90s, and limited services expected. Additionally, Tracy is not feeling well. She had trouble sleeping last night, has a headache, is not hungry, and generally feels like crud.

This would have been a major concern for me in the past, but not now. Tracy is one of the strongest people I know, both physically and mentally. At the beginning of our Northern Tier bicycle trip in 2014, she climbed up the Cascade Mountains with me on the tandem for six and a half hours despite having the flu. She could not eat or drink the entire time. She simply put her head down and pedaled. I still tear up thinking about it. (See our book *Coast*

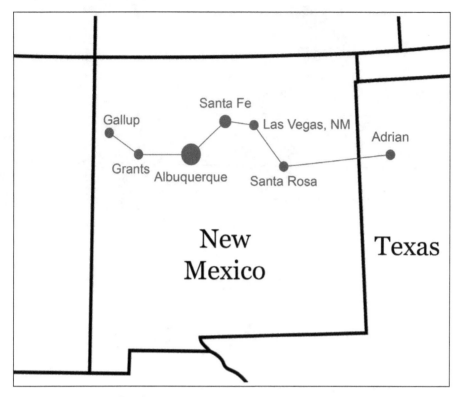

to Coast on a Tandem.)

Since we are uncertain about our pace and how long it will take us to travel between water stops, we fill our foldable water bag for the first time. The extra water adds weight, but almost doubles our water capacity.

We climb steadily out of Adrian before the road flattens, which makes the headwinds seem not quite as bad. We also have cloud cover for the first thirty miles that helps keep the heat somewhat at bay. The frontage road ends four miles past Adrian and we begin riding on the shoulder of I-40. The shoulder is very wide, protected by rumble strips, and in almost perfect condition. Traffic is light on this Saturday morning and the passing trucks, most of which change lanes to give us additional room, actually block some of the relentless headwind and move us along. Soon, the landscape changes and we can tell we are nearing New Mexico.

We arrive at the New Mexico state line twenty-six miles into the ride and stop to take pictures of the "Welcome to New Mexico - Land of Enchantment" sign. Boy, is it beautiful here. The red rock with its many shades and shadows is stunning. One mile down the road, we take our first real break of the day at the Glenrio Welcome Center. We love the look on motorists' faces when we roll up on our bike!

Tracy still does not feel well, but she is hanging in there. She is one tough cookie.

We exit I-40 four miles later and are back on the frontage road. It is much quieter and there is practically no traffic.

Our next stop is the small town of San Jon (pop. 216), where we have lunch at the local gas station, convenience store, and grill. We lost an hour when we crossed the state line and are now on Mountain Time. No wonder the waitress looks at us funny when we order pizza; it's 10 a.m.

The last twenty-four miles to Tucumcari (pop. 4,959) are tough: 92 degrees, rolling hills, and 15-mph headwinds. Despite the difficult riding conditions, the scenery is spectacular, almost outer worldly for two Midwesterners. We tackle the remaining miles by breaking the ride into three eight-mile sections and taking short breaks in between. Although we empty all six of our twenty-four-ounce water bottles on this last stretch, we never have to tap into the water bag. That's fortunate, as the water in the bag likely is well over 100 degrees!

We are staying at the Historic Route 66 Motel on the east end of town tonight. This is a classic 1960s property restored to its original midcentury modern style. The hotel is classic Route 66. The rooms even have the old-style, floor-to-ceiling windows.

Facebook followers

Fran Houser (Owner, Sunflower Station, Adrian, Texas)
Ride safely, my friend!

Paula Roberts
Now you're out of the humidity and into the dry heat!

Peter Flucke
We found the dry heat today - and a 15-mph headwind. Lol

Robyn Stroup
In Tucumcari, Del's Restaurant is pretty good. There is only one grocery store.

Peter Flucke
Thanks for the Intel. Having ice cream at Ken's Ice Cream right now.

The owners are very welcoming. We are here by 1:30 p.m., a little early for check in, but they let us get settled in our room even though they are dealing with a broken hot water pipe that serves the entire motel complex. They apologize for the lack of hot water and assure us it will be fixed soon. We roll the bike into our room (our common practice), and then walk back east a short distance to Ken's Ice Cream for our second lunch of the day. By the time we get back to the hotel, we have hot water.

Robyn, our Warmshowers host from Tulsa, recommended Del's Restaurant for dinner, three blocks west toward town. It is now ninety-six degrees outside with a 22-mph wind out of the southwest. We decide to wait until it cools down a bit before walking the half mile to dinner. Sure glad we are done biking for the day!

Tracy still is not feeling quite right, so she lays down for a nap with her head on the small fleece pillowcase her mother made her for bicycle touring. I think we all want our mothers when we do not feel well. I pass the time by working on our social media and taking a nap myself.

Tracy wasn't feeling well when we pulled into the Historic Route 66 Motel in Tucum-cari, New Mexico. Her head is resting on a fleece pillowcase her mother made for her to take on bike tours.

By 6:30 p.m., Tracy is awake and the temperature has finally started to drop, so we walk to Del's for dinner. The all-you-can-eat salad bar is awesome. After dinner, we stroll through town to see the sights and loosen up our legs before bed.

Tucumcari is a cool little town that has truly embraced all things Route 66. What strikes us most as we walk along admiring the old motels, eateries, gas stations, and curio shops is the abundance of neon lights beckoning to passersby. The neon reds, greens, blues, and whites seem particularly vibrant and appealing in the high desert twilight.

Tomorrow's forecast for our sixty-plus-mile ride to Santa Rosa is 65/91 degrees, winds north 3-5 mph, more climbing, and very few services. Wish us luck!

Day 31
July 3 – Tucumcari to Santa Rosa, New Mexico
64 miles (total miles – 1,727)
Sunny, 80 degrees, light tailwind, beautiful day

Tracy

First, I want to thank everyone for their kind words and well wishes for a speedy recovery. Glad to say I am feeling a lot better today. Thank goodness, because our Adventure Cycling Association map warns us, "Very limited services next 56.9 miles."

After leaving Tucumcari, we bicycle the first twelve miles on I-40. We are getting used to being on the interstate and the semi-truck drivers' beeps and waves continue to make us smile.

Today, we climb at the beginning of the ride and are over 5,000 feet at the highest point. That is about a 1,000-foot elevation gain. The route is mainly along the frontage road after we leave I-40, but we are also on some very nice, but steep, local, and state highways from Cuervo to Santa Rosa.

Facebook followers

Peter Flucke is at The Historic Route 66 Motel, Tucumcari, NM, July 2, 2016
Although we wouldn't trade this experience for anything and are so thankful for the opportunity to share it with all of you, this is not easy! Tracy started the day not feeling well and then had to battle heat and headwinds all day long. She is strong and will recover, but for now she sleeps.

Darlene Luedtke Charles
Praying for a quick recovery. I make a really healthy chicken noodle soup; wish I could send it your way.

Melissa Flucke (Daughter extraordinaire #1)
Feel better mom! I miss you guys!

Yolo Diaz (Leader of Green Bay Go Ride woman's cycling group, medical doctor)
I hope she feels better! Let her rest as much as she needs!

Julie Kolp (Tracy's childhood friend)
Sending good vibes and happy thoughts. Be safe and don't push it. Love you guys.

Gary Smits (Green Bay, Wisconsin bicyclist and Ironman)
You never said it would be easy and we know it is not. You two are a tough package and I give you the utmost respect.

Beth Borman Trost (Peter's high school friend and medical doctor)
Stay strong Tracy! Sleep will hopefully heal you!

Rebecca Cleveland
You captured a prefect "Tired Biker."

Mike Gerke
Have there been many camping opportunities on route 66? Bandit or legit...that bed looks better than a pad/bag.

Peter Flucke
Very few Mike, and with the heat and the headwinds we have been experiencing the AC has been almost a must for us.

Barbara Ali (Former transportation safety manager at Wisconsin Department of Transportation)
What you are doing requires so much of a person. I don't know how you do it at our age and make it seem so easy. I'm proud of both of you and hoping for a full recovery for Tracy.

Peter

Immediately after exiting the interstate, we encounter our first cattle guard blocking Quay County Road Ay. The cattle guard is intended to stop cows from straying onto the freeway from their unfenced pasture while still allowing cars and trucks to cross. Unfortunately, the guard also does a pretty good job of stopping tandem bicycles.

The cattle guard reminds me of a giant storm sewer grate. It consists of a dozen two-inch by two-inch square steel pipes running the width of the road with four-inch gaps in between. The structure is eight-feet wide and sits on top of a concrete vault with stringers to support the pipes. The cattle guard has wings across the road shoulder which prevent the cows (and tandems) from going around the grate.

The cattle guard looks rideable, almost. The four-inch gaps might be manageable on a wide-tired mountain bike, but the tandem's skinny, high-pressure tires would likely bounce uncontrollably. The front tire could even get caught in the gaps and jackknife like on a railroad track, just worse. A crash would be unavoidable and likely catastrophic. We stop, dismount, and push the bike across with me steering and Tracy stabilizing the back. At least we do not have to unload everything.

Today's ride takes us through some very isolated places with little or no services. Our one stop is in the town of Newkirk (pop. 0, yes zero) located at the junction of I-40 and New Mexico State Road 129, about thirty miles in. There is a small convenience store/gas station here, and that is it. We walk into the store to find lunch, restrooms, and fill our water bottles. We find lunch, but the restrooms are out of service and there is no water. Strange. Almost out of water, I ask the older man behind the cramped and cluttered counter where we can fill our bottles. He tells me, in no uncertain terms, that there is no water in Newkirk and that he does not have any for sale. Okay, sorry I asked. (This same thing happened to us the previous year in rural Mississippi while bicycling the length of the Mississippi river, but at least there they had bottled water we could buy.) Hmm, I wonder what will happen if we try to make it the rest of the way in this heat on just soda and Gatorade? Convenience stores everywhere have soda, Gatorade, and bottled water, but not here. (My privilege is showing. It is almost impossible for me to imagine a place in the United States of America, one of the richest countries in the world, where people do not have access to free drinking water. But here I am, again. I am so sad!)

Then, when no other customers are looking, the older man subtly gestures to me to give him our four empty bottles. He slips out a door behind the counter and is gone. A few minutes later the man returns and, without saying a word, hands me the four, full, water bottles. Their weight feels good in my hands. When the store briefly empties the older man, the store owner, tells us that he has his own private supply of drinking water at his residence behind the store. He pays to have the water trucked in, which is why he does not tell people he has water. We offered to pay him, but he waves us off and tells us to

Peter gingerly guides the tandem across the grid of a cattle guard in this image taken from the GoPro camera on Tracy's helmet.

Cattle guards can be bicycle guards, too

"Cattle guards are often used where livestock may graze in open pastures and in between open fence lines. Cattle grids prevent livestock from crossing over property lines and keep them out of dangerous areas. They are a terrific alternative to cattle gates, which require management and maintenance."
(https://www.farmranchstore.com/information)

"If (cows) try to cross the cattle guard, their legs will fall down in between the pipes and they will get stuck. The cattle know this. So, they generally don't try to cross cattle guards."
(https://www.thepioneerwoman.com/home-lifestyle/a15311/the-cattle-guard/)

enjoy our ride and to be careful out there. Thank you, sir, we will do our part. Humanity is an interesting thing.

Before riding into Santa Rosa, we stop at the massive Love's Travel Center for a snack. Boy, is it busy. I think every church group within a fifty-mile radius is here. They are so loud! It probably seems especially loud after being on the bicycle in such a quiet environment all day.

Tracy

The last three miles into Santa Rosa are downhill. We check into our hotel, clean up, and catch the end of the Tour de France bicycle race. We are huge fans of the race and usually watch all twenty-one stages during the month of July. We are suffering from a bit of TDF withdrawal.

A local news reporter left a message on Peter's phone, saying he wants to do an interview about our trip. We try to reach him, but have to leave a message. Hopefully, he will get back to us. (We never do hear back from the

You are looking at the entirety of Newkirk, New Mexico (pop. zero). This small gas station/convenience store offered us a brief respite from the sun, and the owner generously filled our water bottles with some of his private supply.

reporter. Can't blame the guy; it is a Sunday over the holiday weekend.)

Happy Fourth of July to everyone tomorrow. Think of us as we are climbing to Las Vegas, New Mexico.

Day 32
July 4 – Santa Rosa to Las Vegas, New Mexico
64 miles (total miles – 1,791)
Warm, 87 degrees, sunny with a 13-mph headwind

(The next three days were written in Albuquerque on a day off the bike. We did not write them daily as usual due to a combination of long, hard days on the bike, interesting people to visit with, poor connectivity, and the authors being lazy/exhausted.)

Peter

We could not have left Santa Rosa any earlier without riding in the dark. But no complaints, today is going to be a tough one, if we can even pull it off. Our Adventure Cycling map warns us that we'll have: "Very limited services next 96 miles." (Santa Rosa-Santa Fe) We are super-motivated to give it a try.

We are going to be climbing most of the day and it is going to be hot (87 degrees) and dry (15 percent humidity). On top of that, there is a predicted 13-mph headwind, and we will not have any services for the entire sixty-four-mile ride. There isn't even a real town along the way.

To make this work, we need to carry all the food and water needed for the entire day. We have our typical six water bottles, the collapsible water bag (which holds enough water to fill four water bottles), four thirty-two-ounce

Powerades (the electrolytes are important), and a bottle of Sprite. This comes to just about six gallons, and at 8.34 pounds per gallon, we will be carrying an extra fifty pounds. This is the same weight as all the gear we carry. We hate the extra weight because it slows us down and tires us out, especially when climbing, but we cannot afford to run out of liquids. We hope this is enough with an acceptable margin of safety.

Tracy

We reviewed our Adventure Cycling map last night and discovered we had two routes to choose from to Albuquerque. The post-1937 alignment of Route 66, a more direct, flatter, route of 117 miles, or the pre-1937 alignment, which is longer (150 miles), but with less interstate riding, fantastic views, and a more authentic Route 66 feel. Of course, we choose the longer route which has very few services and more climbing to get those fantastic views. So don't feel sorry for us, the tougher route was our choice! We will have several hard climbs today to get from 4,700 feet elevation in Santa Rosa to 6,400 feet in Las Vegas. (This is Las Vegas, New Mexico, not the famous Las Vegas, Nevada, which is almost 700 miles to the west.)

Peter

We are not totally flying without a safety net, though. There is an occasional ranch along the way where we could beg for water, but most of them are well off the road and they all seem to have large, locked gates and even larger dogs! Fortunately, we are riding on Highway 84 for most of the day, and even though it only has two lanes and is in the middle of nowhere, there are a surprising number of vehicles on it. It has a wide shoulder to ride on, and it is actually comforting to see the traffic. Most of the drivers wave as they pass. While we are taking a roadside break, one motorist even starts to pull over and stop near us, presumably to make sure we are okay. When we wave and gave him the thumbs up sign, he smiles, waves, and continues on his way. Nice folks!

Our first possible services are about thirty miles out at the small town of Dilla. There is a lounge/bar here, but it is closed. We stop anyway and take a short break. While we are checking things out, Tracy makes a new friend in a young German Shepherd who wanders over to say hello. He/she is a really

---

Summer is the rainy season in New Mexico

"The wettest months (in New Mexico) are July, August, and early September. This is New Mexico's 'monsoon season,' where moisture laden tropical air triggers frequent, and sometimes violent, afternoon thunderstorms. Lightning associated with these makes summits and ridges especially dangerous, and flash flooding makes camping in dry watercourses unwise."

-Bicycling Route 66 Map 4, Adventure Cycling Association

sweet dog that first sits by Tracy and then follows her around. The dog even follows us down the road a bit when we continue our ride. Tracy finally has to tell the dog to "Go home." It works, although Tracy wishes the dog could come with us. I tell her we do not have water to spare.

Tracy

We reach the city of Romeroville (pop. 13,753) around 1:30 pm and are elated to find an open gas station and Subway. Averaging right around 11 mph, we have used all of the liquids we had with us except for one thirty-two-ounce Powerade. Close!

Peter loves Subway and we head over for lunch and to fill our water bottles. We are the only customers, and the two young women working behind the counter are very interested in our bicycle trip. We talk for a bit and then give them our card to check out the blog. They immediately pull out their phones and look at our blog. I do not think they did any work for the next half hour as we hear them talking about our trip and all the adventures. When we leave, they wish us luck and tell us they will continue to follow our trip. Nice.

Refueled, we pedal the last mile to the Las Vegas (New Mexico) KOA, arriving at 3 p.m., after a long, hard day on the bicycle. We are hot and tired when we arrive, but after a shower and a long nap, we feel more like ourselves.

The air-conditioned campground office also houses the laundry and a small seating area where we hang out, snack, and do chores. We eat dinner at the KOA "restaurant," and tonight is BBQ night. We get a plastic basket filled with fries and barbeque. Coffee or lemonade fill our Styrofoam cups. Simple, but it sure tastes good. After dinner, we wander around the campground and visit with a very nice couple from Albuquerque. They have an RV in which they just take off and see where they end up. Sounds like fun to us.

The temperature is starting to drop. It should be a great night for sleeping with clear skies, a slight breeze, and a predicted low of 55 degrees. The night

The outdoor restaurant at the KOA campground in Las Vegas, New Mexico, featured BBQ night when we arrived on the Fourth of July, 2016.

Facebook followers

Peter Flucke is at Las Vegas, New Mexico, KOA Journey. July 4, 2016
Camping tonight at elevation (6,400').

Barbara Ali
Not what I imagined for Vegas. Where's the buffet?

Peter Flucke
Right! And honestly, we could kill a buffet right now!

Greg Cribb (JB Cycle & Sport mechanic and Peter's road riding partner)
Next comes the mountains! Getting closer to AZ.

Paul Knickelbine (Peter's high school classmate)
Great work. Is that the pass elevation?

Peter Flucke
Not yet Paul. Heading to 7,800' in the near future.

---

sky is amazing, with many stars to see. We can hear the fireworks from town, but unfortunately cannot see them.

Day 33
July 5 – Las Vegas to Santa Fe, New Mexico
74 miles (total miles – 1,865)
Hot, 90 degrees, sunny and 15-mph headwind

Tracy

Fortunately, we went to bed early last night (9 p.m.) and slept very well in the cool (55 degrees), dry (12 percent humidity) mountain air (6,400 feet). We are up well before sunrise, and with our headlamps on, we eat breakfast, break camp, and get everything back on the bicycle. Typically, this takes us about an hour, but we are out of practice. So this being the first time really camping on this trip, an hour and a half later we are finally ready to go.

We leave the Las Vegas (New Mexico) KOA campground at sunrise and immediately start climbing and falling, and climbing and falling ... It is a hell of a way to wake up. Unlike yesterday, we have services available throughout the ride, so we do not have to carry a full day's supply of water and food with us. Yes, less weight on the bicycle.

Our route today from Las Vegas takes us south, west, then north around the Sangre de Cristo Mountains, the southernmost subrange of the Rocky Mountains. We are riding on the frontage road to I-25/84 south. This is the

Santa Fe Trail
A brief history

"Between 1821 and 1880, the Santa Fe Trail was primarily a commercial highway connecting Missouri and Santa Fe, New Mexico. The route was pioneered by Missouri trader William Becknell ... Not surprisingly, others got into the trade soon after Becknell, and by 1825 goods from Missouri were not only being traded in Santa Fe, but to other points farther south as well.

"From 1821 until 1846, the Santa Fe Trail was a two-way international commercial highway used by both Mexican and American traders. Then, in 1846, the Mexican-American War began... After the Treaty of Guadalupe Hidalgo ended the war in 1848, the Santa Fe Trail became a national road connecting the more settled parts of the United States to the new southwest territories. Commercial freighting along the trail boomed to unheard-of levels, ... The trail was also used by stagecoach lines, thousands of gold seekers heading to the California and Colorado gold fields, adventurers, missionaries, wealthy New Mexican families, and emigrants.

"In 1866, just a year after the Civil War ended, an unprecedented period of railroad expansion began in the new state of Kansas... by 1873, two different rail lines reached from eastern Kansas all the way into Colorado. ... the Atchison, Topeka, and Santa Fe Railroad, reached the top of Raton Pass (at the Colorado-New Mexico border) in late 1878... Then, in February 1880, the railroad reached Santa Fe, and the trail faded into history."
(https://www.nps.gov/safe/learn/historyculture/index.htm)

route of the old Santa Fe Trail as well as historic Route 66.

Nineteen miles into the ride, we drop down to the Pecos River at 6,000 feet of elevation and then begin a thirteen-mile climb back up to 6,800 feet. It's not a steep climb, just a long one.

Peter

We stop at the Pecos River Station, a gas station/convenience store a mile west of the Pecos River, for a rest, snack, and water. An old cowboy sitting at a picnic table in the shade of the covered front porch is opening pull tabs. The contrasts with Tracy standing by our bike, leaning against the wall near the front door just behind him, are many. The dark and weathered-skinned cowboy is wearing a wide-brimmed, brown felt, cowboy hat, long-sleeved denim work shirt, blue jeans, and scuffed cowboy boots. Tracy, on the other hand, with her long blonde hair pulled back in a ponytail and pale skin, has just removed her light-colored, plastic and foam bicycle helmet, and is wearing a neon-colored, polka dot, high-tech, short-sleeved biking jersey, padded bicycle shorts, and bicycle shoes with Velcro closures. Next to the cowboy on a large pole supporting the roof of the porch is an old phone booth. On the cowboy's hip is a modern cellphone. Tracy has the tandem, I wonder where the cowboy's horse is? I smile to myself as I walk into the store.

Seventeen miles more and we pass the entrance to the Pecos National Historical Park Visitor Center. We would love to stop and explore, but what we would love even more is to get out of the heat and wind, and have a real meal.

We stop for lunch about twenty miles later at a small Tex-Mex cantina in Pecos. Eating all of my huge burrito with green chili sauce could have been a problem, but I opted to only eat half of it and everything worked out fine.

Tracy

After lunch, we climb from 6,800 to 7,600 feet in five miles to the town of Glorieta. We then bounce up and down until our ending point in Santa Fe at about 7,000 feet. We get into Santa Fe (pop. 83,579) at 4 p.m. and immediately get lost. We are hot and tired from a long hard day of riding. My mind is not working well, and I am struggling to navigate. We had planned to check out some of the attractions in town suggested by our Warmshowers hosts, but are just too tired to figure out how to get there.

As luck would have it, Second Street Brewery is on route to our hosts' house, so we stop in to have a beer, a snack, and get a commemorative glass.

Peter

Somewhat refreshed, we hop on the Santa Fe Rail Trail, just outside the brewery, for the five-mile ride to our Warmshowers stay. The trail is great! It runs along a now-dry riverbed, and best of all, it is all downhill! We are there in no time and in a much better mood.

Our hosts (Dennis and Patty) live in a beautiful southwestern-style condominium. We arrive at 5 p.m., but expectedly, no one is home yet. Not to worry, we have the code to the garage door and let ourselves in. Our room is made up and there are fresh towels on the bed. We shower and make ourselves at home as instructed.

Dennis arrives home first, followed by Patty after her yoga class. I am jealous. I love yoga and usually practice twice a week when we are home. We have a lovely dinner of salad, fresh fruit, and pizza.

We stay up way too late talking. We really enjoy the company. One of our biggest regrets about doing home stays is that we never seem to have enough time to get to know our hosts. Fortunately, many of them have become life-long friends.

Tracy

I wish we had the time and energy to explore Santa Fe. This is one more place we will add to our "We need to get back here someday" list.

Day 34
July 6 – Santa Fe to Albuquerque, New Mexico
74 miles (total miles – 1,939)
Warm, 89 degrees, sunny, light crosswind/headwind

Tracy

We are up at 5:15 a.m. to hit the road at sunrise. Our Adventure Cycling map again warns us, "Very limited services next 96 miles." Patty and Dennis set out a nice breakfast for us, and with full stomachs we are on the road by 6:15 a.m. Last night, Dennis gave us directions to get out of town and back on route so we could miss road construction on Highway 14, the Turquoise Trail National Scenic Byway and our route to Albuquerque. His directions are spot on. They even give us an up-close and personal view of a life-size Brontosaurus family of three on the 1.8-mile-long Dinosaur Trail, which winds unobtrusively (except for the dinosaurs) through a residential neighborhood. Too funny.

The first fifteen miles are downhill, followed by a three-mile uphill to Madrid, a nice way to start the day. Dennis suggested we check out Madrid, describing it as a historic coal mining and ghost town. It is now a hippy enclave and artist community, with lots of cool shops and restaurants. Unfortunately, the only shop open is Java Junction, so we stop for pastries and lattes. It looks like an interesting town to spend some time in.

Peter

All too soon we are back on the bike for the monster climb out of Madrid. This is a tough one! Twelve hundred feet in less than five miles, and then another 500-foot climb on top of that. I am sure Tracy is singing *The Elephant Song* in her head, "One elephant went out to play, up on a spider's web one day, he had such enormous fun that he asked another elephant to come," etc. At the top, she tells me she got up to forty elephants during the climb. My song is *100 Bottles of Beer on the Wall*. I got down to thirty-two bottles, but we made it. We hit 40 mph a couple of times going downhill on the backside. (I tell Tracy we are going 25 mph. I always do, and she seems

Turquoise Trail National Scenic Byway

"Nestled in the hills and valleys of central New Mexico, it is one of the state's most interesting and scenic drives. ... This often-forgotten road is filled with history, scenic views, ghost towns, a national forest, a ski resort, art galleries, shops, museums, and more.

"Linking New Mexico's two major cities – Santa Fe and Albuquerque, the 65-mile national scenic byway is often called the back road between the two cities. Named for the rich turquoise deposits found near its northern end, the Turquoise Trail was used for centuries by Native Americans and Spanish explorers before miners began to flood the area in the late 1800s in search of the hills' many rich minerals. The beautiful blue-green turquoise was first mined by the early Pueblo people as early as 900 A.D. Though this hilly highway has seen much recent growth, it still maintains a historic view of the Old West, along with its galleries, restaurants, and museums."
(https://www.legendsofamerica.com/nm-turquoisetrail/)

happy with that.)

We climb again going into San Antonito as we skirt the Sandia Mountains to the west. Thankfully, this time I only make it into the seventies of the beer song. We have lunch in San Antonito and then coast the next thirty miles into Albuquerque (pop. 559,350).

Tracy

The bike route through Albuquerque is easy to follow, mostly on bike lanes and all downhill. We enjoy the ten miles of city riding to our hotel in Old Town on the far west side. Our route takes us through the University of New Mexico. We had been here four years ago on a track and field recruiting visit with our youngest daughter, Alexandra. The university was interested in Alex pole vaulting for them, but she decided to vault for the University of Minnesota instead.

About five miles from our hotel, we stop along the side of a city street to rehydrate and check our map. Suddenly, a baby hummingbird flies right into our bike. He lands by the rear tire and sits there chirping. I want to save him. After a few minutes he seems to regain his strength and flies to the top of one of the front panniers. I take a picture. Eventually, he flies into some near-

Facebook follower

Patrick Kolp (motorcycle tourist)
When are you going to hit the hot weather?

Peter Flucke
When? Dude, it was 98 here yesterday! Seriously though, not sure. We are just taking it one day, one mile, at a time.

Patrick Kolp
Just checking, we hit 106 (in the Mojave Desert). I know it's night and day different but that was hot the breeze was hot the wind was hot. So on a bike it feels twice as hot.

by bushes and continues to chirp. What a great chance encounter.

Peter

We walk the bike into the lobby of the Hotel Albuquerque Old Town and check in. This always feels funny to me, but no one ever seems to care. It is a beautiful property and within walking distance of food, shopping, and the New Mexico Museum of Natural History and Science.

Shortly after checking into the hotel, we get a phone call from Mitch Porter (remember that last name). He is a friend of our Tulsa Warmshowers host, Robyn. Robyn told Mitch we were coming to town, and Mitch called with an offer to take us to a microbrewery for a beer. Yes, please! He takes us to the

Showered and refreshed after a hot day on the bike, nothing tastes better than a microbrew (or in Tracy's case, a Diet Coke). This time it's at Bow & Arrow Brewery in Albuquerque, New Mexico.

Bow & Arrow Brewery a short distance away. Mitch is a fish biologist and meeting some colleagues there. One colleague just happens to be part owner of the brewery. We spend a couple of hours talking natural resources, beer, and of course, drinking a few as well.

Tracy

The Bow and Arrow Brewery is new, and staff members are still following their employee manual: "No one gets served without a valid ID." Crap, my ID is back at the hotel, so no beer for me. I was so looking forward to a hearty dark beer. I guess a Diet Coke will have to do.

Later, Mitch drops us off at the Church Street Cafe in Old Town for dinner, after which we walk back to the hotel and call it a night. What a day! Tomorrow we will explore Albuquerque more.

Facebook followers

Peter Flucke is with Tracy Flucke at Bow & Arrow Brewing Co.
Albuquerque, New Mexico - July 6, 2016
Look what we found in ABQ!

Ann Evans Dettlaff
That looks more like it.

Darlene Luedtke Charles
NOW THAT'S LIVIN'! Enjoy every minute of it. You both deserve a little pampering.

Heather Lindsley
Now that looks refreshing!

Rebecca Lyn
Did you have to buy the civilian clothes or do you carry them in your bags?

Peter Flucke
The civvies are ours. Lol

Elisa Pitrof (Peter's high school girlfriend)
I see the beer radar is still working well!

Peter Flucke
And now, the rest of the story; Tracy Flucke forgot her ID and (at age 54) they wouldn't serve her. That's not really her beer, I borrowed it for her and had to give it back. I had two, just so she wouldn't feel bad.

Mary Jane Clements Quass
Well Tracy, if ya got it flaunt it.

Day 35
July 7 – Albuquerque New Mexico
0 miles (total miles – 1,939)
Beautiful, sunny, 95 degrees

Peter

We got up when we felt like it this morning at the Hotel Albuquerque Old Town. The hotel is a classic southwestern style and very comfortable. Our room has a corner window with a commanding view to the north, west and south, and a king-sized bed. This is quite a change from our little two-person tent, although we love them both. We hit the streets after breakfast to pick up

If it seems as though Peter is wearing this shirt in a lot of photos, you're right. We only had room for two sets of street clothes and two sets of biking clothes apiece.

Sandia Peak Tramway

"With 2.7 miles in horizontal length, the Sandia Peak Tramway is officially the world's longest passenger tramway. Launching from the Lower Terminal at 6,559 feet and rising to the Upper Terminal at 10,378 feet, the tramway rises a total of 3,819 feet with the support of just two towers. This means that in addition to being the world's longest passenger tramway, Sandia Peak also has one of the longest clear spans: the distance between Tower 2 and the Upper Terminal is 1.5 miles. This impressive engineering feat is one of the most visited attractions in Albuquerque, and the tramway attracts more than 250,000 passengers each year.

"Located in the Cibola National Forest, the Sandia Peak Tramway was constructed from 1964 to 1966 for a total cost of $2 million. This included 5,000 helicopter trips needed to construct Tower 2 (the higher tower) and install the cabling. To ensure your safety, the hefty tramway track ropes weigh 52 tons and are about 1.5 inches in diameter. To keep things moving at a normal speed of 13.6 miles per hour, this double reversible passenger aerial tramway is driven by a 600-horsepower electric motor.

"While the terminals and towers are still original, new tram cars were added for the 20th anniversary in 1986. And yes, that means the Sandia Peak Tramway is now more than 50 years old. These new tram cars each have a capacity of 10,000 pounds or 50 passengers. They'll take you each length of your trip in 14 minutes, and you have the option to spend as much time as you'd like at the top, whether you'd like to do a quick round-trip visit or stay up high and enjoy multiple hiking trails from the Upper Terminal." (https://www.outdoorproject.com/united-states/new-mexico/sandia-peak-tramway)

supplies and explore.

Late morning, we take an Uber to the Sandia Peak Aerial Tramway. The ride to the top is spectacular and the views of Albuquerque and the surrounding mountains are well worth the trip.

Tracy

We head back to the hotel for lunch, work on social media, and wash the bike. The old girl is holding up really well! After a mandatory nap, we walk over to the Ponderosa Brewery to have a beer and plan out our next several days. Tex-Mex for dinner again, and then back to our room to pack. We cannot wait to get back to Albuquerque someday. We have really enjoyed our stay!

> **Facebook follower**
>
> **Patrick Kolp**
> Stay safe and hydrated. You have lots of hot temps ahead.

Day 36
July 8 – Albuquerque to Grants, New Mexico
80 miles (total miles – 2,019)
Sunny, 87 degrees, tailwind in the morning, head/crosswind in afternoon

Tracy

We watch the sun rise over the Sandi Mountains from our Albuquerque hotel room as we eat breakfast. We are up early to get on the road by 6:30 a.m. The air is cool and wind is calm. The first two miles of our ride brings us to the Paseo del Basque Trail, Albuquerque's premiere multi-use trail which goes from the north to the south edges of the metro area through the Rio Grande's cottonwood bosque (forest). In less than a mile, the trail drops us off on Route 66 and the Rio Bravo Bridge. Once we cross the river, we start to climb what the locals refer to as Nine Mile Hill.

Peter

Nine Mile Hill is, in fact, exactly nine miles long. I know because I measured it with our bicycle computer. Needless to say, we are warmed up by the time we reach the top. The view from the "hill" is worth the climb, though. Picture postcard New Mexico!

Our route now has us back on the shoulder of I-40 for twenty-plus miles. Again, the shoulder is wide, mostly clean, and the motorists are exceptionally accommodating of our presence. We have many long descents (one over 45 mph) and the views do not disappoint. The only issue we have is our second flat tire of the trip (the rear, of course) about ten miles down the freeway. A small wire from a retread truck tire has stuck in the tire and penetrated the tube. We are back on the road twenty minutes later; pretty quick for a fully loaded tandem rear tire change.

We stop for a break a few miles down the road at the 66 Pit Stop. The gas station/convenience store is very much like a Love's, and we are told they are a local chain. It is nice to be able to wash our hands. Our next stop is at the Villa De Cubero Trading Post eleven miles further on.

Tracy

The end of our day is spent traveling on Highway 124/historic Route 66. The road is in great shape and provides amazing views of the beautiful multi-colored rock formations. We are now traveling through several pueblos, including Laguna and Acoma. We do not stop to tour the pueblos, but are able to see some from the road. Amazing.

We are now to the Pueblo Alternate section of our Adventure Cycling maps. We can choose to bicycle an extra five-mile loop with a massive climb to Sky City, the Sky City Cultural Center, and Haak'u Museum, or not. As much as we would like to check these out, we just do not have time, and the

Villa De Cubero Trading Post

"Shortly after the realignment of Route 66 (1937), Wallace and Mary Gunn relocated their business to the new alignment. Called the Villa De Cubero Trading Post, the complex grew to include a service station, cafe, and a small tourist court. The villa became popular with celebrities such as Dezi and Lucy Arnez, Vivian Vance, and the Von Trapp family. Reportedly, Ernest Hemmingway resided in the small tourist court for two weeks while working on *The Old Man and the Sea*. Mary Gunn ran the café across the street from the trading post from 1941 to 1972.

"Though the café and tourist courts are closed, the trading post still caters to Route 66 travelers today, operating as a convenience store and gas station." https://www.legendsofamerica.com/nm-66ghosttowns/

Pueblo is the Spanish word for village

"Spanish explorers used the word "pueblo" to describe both permanent residential structures and the people living in these communities throughout the middle Rio Grande Valley. When the Spanish arrived in 1540, there were possibly more than 100 pueblos located along the Rio Grande Valley, from northern Taos Pueblo to southern Isleta Pueblo. Today there are 19 pueblos in New Mexico, each with its own government but sharing a common prehistory and culture."
https://www.nps.gov/petr/planyourvisit/pueblos.htm

"New Mexico contains the largest number of federally recognized Pueblo communities in the United States. Pueblo communities are happy to welcome visitors to experience their culture and traditions. But ask they contact the pueblo directly to ensure it is open to visitors."
https://indianpueblo.org/new-mexicos-19-pueblos/

climb to Sky City seems a bit daunting in this energy-zapping heat. This is one more place we will add to our "We need to get back here someday" list.

We bicycled through Laguna, Acoma, and Zuni Pueblos, and the Ramah Navajo Nation.

Peter

We stop at our second 66 Pit Stop of the day in Laguna and discover they are also the home of the world-famous Laguna Burger. (We've never heard of it.) We wisely pass on the burger with twenty-three miles to go, and the wind and heat increasing.

Closer to Grants (pop. 9,106), the rock becomes black as we are entering the lava fields from the eruption of Mount Taylor over 10,000 years ago. It is very strange to see this type of rock in New Mexico. But just as in Hawaii, there is beauty in its simplicity and starkness.

We stop for a short break and snack at a convenience store just east of Grants. The store is unremarkable, but the giant pumice rock and petrified log near the entrance are very cool. We are looking forward to bicycling through Petrified Forest National Park in Arizona in four days and appreciate the preview. We also discover from our map that the Great Divide Mountain Bike Trail crosses near the store. The trail is a really tough off-road ride, not conducive to travel by a road tandem touring team.

We are staying at a Days Inn in Grants tonight. Dinner is at Denny's, believe it or not. At least we get a fifteen percent discount on the bill with our AARP card. This is not your grandparents AARP!

Day 37
July 9 – Grants to Ramah, New Mexico
47 miles (total miles – 2,066)
Warm, 87 degrees, sunny, headwind

Peter

We take full advantage of the Days Inn free "breakfast." While we eat, we start up a conversation with two young men and discover they are part of a trio biking the Great Divide Mountain Bike Route from Canada to Mexico. They are beat up! Besides the obvious stress and strain of their 2,700-mile journey, they had ALL crashed, at 35 mph, about a week ago and at least two of them ended up in the hospital: one concussion and lots of road rash. They had finished their ride on the trail for the day and were cruising downhill on a paved road into town for the night when they overlapped wheels. Poor bastards, they weren't even on the trail when it happened. We feel really badly for them, but they are back on their bikes and will be finishing their ride in just three more days. Stuff happens!

From Grants, we descend slightly for about two miles and then start to climb again.

Tracy

We are going a bit shorter today because we want to check out some cool places along the route. Our ride takes us through two national monuments - El Malpais National Monument and Conservation Area (encompassing 178 federally protected square miles) and El Morro National Monument and Conservation Area (encompassing two square miles). Both look like they will be amazing and we cannot wait to travel through them.

Peter

We arrive at El Malpais National Monument around 10 a.m. and start to explore. Our first stop on this volcanic landscape is a cauldron by the same name. The park has many natural features left behind by the volcano, including lava beds, sink holes, and lava tubes. There is lots of caving done in this area in the ancient lava tubes.

Our next stop, after more climbing, is one of the monument's visitor centers. Besides friendly staff and information, they have cold-filtered WATER! Yummy. We meet a very nice law enforcement ranger. With my law enforcement and park ranger background, we hit it off and I enjoy our conversation. The ranger tells us many ancient artifacts are found in the area because indigenous peoples used the lava formations as shelter. All artifacts are federally protected. All too soon, Tracy must remind me we need to keep moving.

Tracy

About four miles down the road, we decide to check out the privately owned Ice Cave and Bandera Volcano. It looks like a fun place to tour, but we

El Malpais National Conservation Area

"The El Malpais National Conservation Area (NCA) was established in 1987 to protect nationally significant geological, archaeological, ecological, cultural, scenic, scientific, and wilderness resources surrounding the Zuni-Bandera volcanic field. El Malpais translates to 'the badlands' in Spanish.

"The NCA includes dramatic sandstone cliffs, canyons, La Ventana Natural Arch, Chain of Craters Back Country Byway, Joe Skeen Campground, the Narrows Picnic Area, and the Cebolla and West Malpais Wilderness Areas. There are many opportunities for photography, hiking, camping, and wildlife viewing within this unique NCA.

"For more than 10,000 years people have interacted with the El Malpais landscape. Historic and prehistoric sites provide connections to the past. More than mere artifacts, these cultural resources are kept alive by the spiritual and physical presence of contemporary Native American groups, including the Ramah Navajo and Puebloan peoples of Acoma, Laguna, and Zuni. These tribes continue their ancestral uses of El Malpais including gathering plant materials, paying respect, and renewing ties." https://www.nps.gov/elma

are finding it difficult to get there by bicycle. First, we have a two-mile climb to the attraction. Unfortunately, the climb is not the hard part of reaching this natural wonder. As it turns out, the entrance road is not paved. Hell, it isn't even gravel. Now, if you lived on an extinct volcano, what would you use to surface your half-mile-long, hilly, entrance road? You've got it, volcanic ash! It may be drivable in a car, but it sure isn't bikeable. This is a first for us. So, push the bike we do!

After stopping at the visitor center, we hike twenty minutes up to the edge of the volcano crater. The view is both beautiful and desolate. Well worth the time, although at about 8,000 feet we definitely can feel the effects of the altitude. The volcano erupted over 10,000 years ago and is one of the largest volcanos in the region. From Look Out Point, visitors can see fifteen other volcanos out of the twenty-nine in the region.

Back down from the volcano, we take the short hike to the ice cave. This is crazy! Forty to fifty feet down into the cave it is 31 degrees year-round, and there is an ice pool that is twenty-four feet thick. Some of the ice dates back 3,400 years. The ice is tinted green from an Arctic alga. Experts have no idea how the algae got to New Mexico; it typically is only found in the Arctic. https://www.icecaves.com/

After our tours, we push the bicycle back to the highway and ride the last half mile to the Continental Divide (7,882 feet). This is the highest we have ever been on our bicycle and we can feel the lack of oxygen. The rest of the day's ride is pretty much downhill, but unfortunately, we have a nasty head-wind to deal with and must work hard to keep the bicycle moving, even on the downhill.

Peter

Our overnight stay is at the El Morro RV Park and Cabins, which is located one mile east of El Morro National Monument and Conservation Area. We will have to wait until tomorrow to check out this national monument.

The campground is pretty standard, but the Ancient Way Café adjacent to the campground is quite the pleasant surprise. The café looks like any little eclectic café you might find at 7,200 feet in western New Mexico, but who would have suspected they have a gourmet chef and baker? This is the best real meal we have had in months. After dinner, we walk across the street to the organic grocery store to pick up some goodies for breakfast.

The campground staff is very nice and welcoming, and we enjoy our stay. This is only our second time camping. The heat and lack of campgrounds are definitely limiting our ability to camp.

As we prepare to climb into our tent for the night, we have the pleasure of listening to two owls calling to each other while we gaze at a crystal-clear sky with twinkling stars. At over 7,000 feet, we feel like we can almost touch the stars, they are so bright. Soon, the moon's brightness will obscure many of those stars. This has been one of the best days of our journey.

Day 38
July 10 – Ramah to Gallup, New Mexico
61 miles (total miles – 2,127)
Sunny, warm, 87 degrees, headwind early and then tailwind

Tracy

The stars are still out and the owls are calling again as we break camp. We

El Morro National Monument and Conservation Area

"For centuries, those who traveled ... stopped to camp at the shaded oasis found here. On the rock, they left evidence of their passing – symbols, names, dates, and fragments of their stories carved in the stone. El Morro is the site of over 2,000 petroglyphs. It also was one of the most reliable water sources in the area, the pool at El Morro has been drawing people to its banks for hundreds of years. Ancestral Puebloans, Spanish explorers and American emigrants all found respite in its waters." https://www.nps.gov/elmo

eat a delicious breakfast of homemade wheat bread, peanut butter, and dried fruit from the organic grocery store. Two of the neighbors' chickens even join us for breakfast. We are packed up and on the bicycle by 6:30 a.m., and are pleased to be getting a nice early start. It is cool out, 60 degrees, so we don our jackets before leaving. Our plan is to stop at the El Morro National Monument and Conservation Area this morning as it is only a couple of miles down the road. We are excited to explore this unique park.

Peter

After only 1.24 miles of riding, and as we are approaching the sign for El Morro National Monument, I suddenly hear and feel the rear derailleur cable snap. Twang, like a guitar string. Oh, $#/+!

"Did you hear that?" I ask Tracy.

"What was it?" she replies.

"That would be the sound of our rear derailleur cable snapping."

"Really?"

"Yup."

We pull to the shoulder to assess the situation. Sure enough, the cable has snapped just inside the shifter. Fortunately, we have been carrying an extra cable for over fifteen years, just in case. Unfortunately, I have never actually changed one before, certainly not sixty miles from any city and something like 200 miles from the nearest bike shop. I will be forced to "tie off" the derailleur in one gear if I cannot replace the cable. But which gear to choose? A larger gear will allow us to go fast downhill, but will make it almost impossible to climb all but the slightest grades. A smaller gear, on the other hand, will allow us to climb, but we will not be able to take advantage of the downhills, or even travel at our normal speeds on the flats. Fixing the derailleur in one gear will allow us to move, but at a much slower average pace. The predicted heat and wind building later in the day means we do not want to be on the road any longer than absolutely necessary. This could become dangerous quickly. Nothing to do but try and fix the cable. It is our best option.

The first challenge is finding and removing the old cable end, located somewhere inside the shifter. This is no easy task because the sun is so bright

Peter works on our broken rear derailleur cable in a spot conveniently situated for this photo. It was the first time we ever had to make this repair and offered a good example of the value of having basic bike mechanic skills. You never know when or where you might need them.

that, even with my sunglasses on, my pupils are so restricted I cannot see into the deep, dark recesses of the shifter. Eventually, after moving the bike's handlebars into the precious little shade offered by the park sign, using the flashlight on my phone, and constantly wiping sweat out of my eyes, I find it! Now we know where it is. The second task is to thread the new cable through the Shimano 105, 10-speed shifter.

"How the hell do I get this thing around the bend?"

Eventually, I figure out there is a tiny pilot hole you feed the cable out of, and then back into. How about that. The rest of the installation is relatively easy. We Did It!

Tracy

We are literally making the repair in the sliver of shade of the El Morro National Monument sign. Unfortunately, this is as close as we get to the park. After an hour and a half, and without a single car going by, we reluctantly continue our ride to Gallup.

Our map warns us, "Limited services next 117 miles." We are traveling through the Ramah Navajo Nation, Zuni Pueblo, and Navajo Indian Reservation today. Services are indeed very limited but, between an occasional gas station and a Family Dollar store, we find enough to get by.

(On a recent trip to visit our youngest daughter in Texas, we detoured to spend a few days in Tulsa, Oklahoma, with some good friends and were able to meet up with our Tulsa Warmshowers host, Robyn. We had a great visit and shared stories about our stay in 2016. Robyn shared a great one about her partner, Mike, and how he followed us on our Route 66 trip using our From the Finish Line tracker. Each morning, he would get up and check on our progress and link the view to the TV in the living room to watch us travel throughout the day. On the morning of July 10, 2016, Robyn walked into the living room to find Mike frantic. He told her that our dot had not moved for several hours. He explained that when he zoomed in to see where we were, it was in the middle of nowhere.

"We need to call the police to check on them, now!" he told Robyn.

Ha-ha! Sorry we scared you, Mike. They followed us via the tracker all the way to Santa Monica, California.)

Peter

After the repair, we drop like a stone downhill to a convenience store in Ramah, twelve miles down the road, where we fill our water bottles and buy a snack. Back on the road, we continue our descent, our reward for a job well done. We descended from 7,200 feet to 6,500 feet, but now we are climbing back to 7,200 feet. Really! To make matters worse, we are still heading west and have picked up a nasty (15-plus mph) headwind. At times, it feels like we are going backward. Again, REALLY!

All of these ups and downs (literally) have given me the opportunity to run through the bike's full range of gears, and something is not quite right. While the bike is shifting smoothly, the gear range seems to be off. Emboldened by my recent cable repair, we pull to the side of the road and within a couple of minutes, I have Violet shifting perfectly again.

Luckily, our route turns north twenty-five miles into the ride onto Highway 602 toward Gallup, our ending point for the day, thirty-five miles away. At least now we have a cross and slight tailwind. It is a nice change. Unfortunately, the first nine miles of Highway 602 features another climb of 700 feet to an elevation of approximately 7,300 feet. (Haven't we been here before?) From this point until we get to Gallup, we bounce up and down and finish with a last little climb into town.

Tracy

There are a fair number of drivers on this two-lane road, but they are good about giving us space as they pass. One woman passes us, beeps, and gives us a friendly wave on her way by. I wave back. A few minutes later, we stop along the side of the road for a short break to prepare for our final push into Gallup. As we are eating a snack and hydrating, I see the car with the friendly woman go by again, this time in the opposite direction. She makes a U-turn and pulls onto the shoulder behind us.

Peter says, "Oh, oh, what's going on here?"

I tell Peter it is okay; I saw her pass before and we waved to each other. Peter did not see this interaction from the front of the bicycle.

The woman gets out of her car and walks our way. She explains that she wanted to stop on her first pass, but saw her uncle walking along the road and had to stop and pick him up. She tells us that few people on the reservation have cars and if you see a family member walking, you have to give them a ride. After dropping off her uncle, she decided to come back and find out what we are all about. She has never seen a bicycle for two people before. She is very interested in our bicycle, gear, where we are from, etc. We talk for a bit and then she wishes us luck, gets back in her car, and heads down the road. I am so glad she decided to stop and chat.

Peter

It takes us a while to find a hotel in Gallup. We finally opt for a Hilton Garden Inn with a great rate near the freeway. Staying near the freeway happens a lot. At least at the Hilton, we have a shower, laundry, food, and a comfortable bed. All much needed. It has been a hell of a day!

Facebook followers

Peter Flucke is at El Morro RV Park, Cabins/Ancient Way Cafe. Ramah, NM
July 10, 2016
We had a visitor for breakfast! (The chickens.)

Nathan Vandervest (our trainer from Bellin Health Fitness Center, Green Bay)
Did you eat him?

Peter Flucke
Not enough time. Lol

Patrick Kolp
Did you have eggs or chicken?

Peter Flucke
Peanut butter and homemade bread. Ha!

John Z. Wetmore
You will never have a late start for your ride if you have roosters waking you up at the first light of dawn.

Elisa Pitrof
Great when a negative experience turns into a positive learning experience for you! So glad all worked out well!

Peter Flucke
Us too!

Richard C. Moeur
If you haven't already, at least visit the El Rancho Hotel's lobby.

Steve McCurdy (Peter's high school friend)
You are responsible for *Route 66* by Bobby Troupe constantly going through my head. Thanks! Lol

---

Chapter 8

State of
Arizona

July 11-July 19, 2016
387 miles/2,514 total

Day 39
July 11 – Gallup, New Mexico, to Chambers, Arizona
52 miles (total miles – 2,179)
Sunny, 85 degrees, 25 mph headwind

Peter

With only fifty miles to go to Chambers, Arizona, we sleep in until 6:30 a.m. and are on the road by 8 a.m. The temperature is in the low 60s and there is a very light west wind.

Reluctantly, we pedal west out of Gallup. I say reluctantly because we have not really given the city a fair chance. Between the broken derailleur cable, hills, and nasty headwind yesterday, we just did not have it in us to explore last night or this morning.

We are heading to Chambers, Arizona (pop. 640) today, not because it is anything special, but because of where it is located. Chambers is only twenty-two miles east of Petrified Forest National Park, and we are planning to bike the twenty-eight-mile road through the park. If we tried to do the ride all in one day, it would be a seventy-four-mile day to the beginning of the park road and 102 miles to the end of it. And unfortunately, there is no lodging in or near the park. The next lodging is in Holbrook, nineteen miles further down the road for a grand total of 121 miles from Gallup.

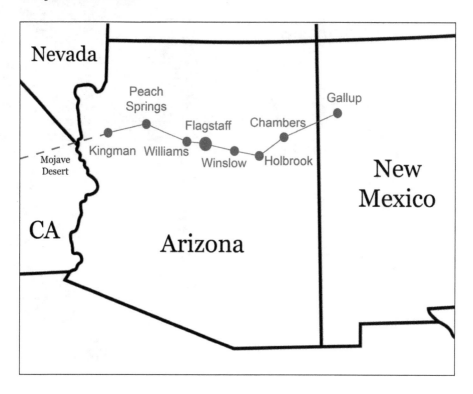

This would not leave us time to explore the park, and we would be exhausted, if we even made it. So, Chambers it is. Located on the edge of the Navajo Indian Reservation, Chambers has a gas station, hotel, and restaurant according to our map. However, the addendum to the map says there is only a restaurant in town. We are hoping for the best.

Tracy

Too late, we learned we missed the cool, historic, section of Gallup. We were not impressed with the part of the city we saw; it was pretty run-down looking. Evidently, when we turned left (west) on historic Route 66 into town last night, we should have turned right instead. Oh well, that's the life of a cross-country bicyclist. Sometimes things are only a few miles away or in the other direction, and you totally miss them. I guess we will have to come back to Gallup someday and really give it a chance.

Our ride today begins with us bicycling west on Highway 118, which parallels I-40 for twenty-three miles to the Arizona state line. The road becomes the interstate frontage road in Arizona. Navigation is pretty straight forward even though we frequently cross over and under the freeway. We must cross, because Highway 118 and the frontage road are not continuous on either side of the freeway. In fact, we have to be sure to cross at the points designated on our map or run the risk of riding down the road three/four miles only to discover that the road just ends. It would be nice if there were DEAD END signs, but no such luck.

Shortly before leaving New Mexico, we are having trouble figuring out if we should cross under the highway or stay on the side we are on. Of course, there are no street signs, but the distance we have traveled to the crossover is correct. We are standing on the side of the road trying to decide what to do when a big yellow Caterpillar front end loader comes down the street. I flag down the driver to ask for help.

He pulls over, shuts off the engine, and climbs down. His name is Oscar, and he works for the McKinley County Road Department. Obviously, he knows exactly where we are. Oscar is very helpful and gets us going in the right direction. He also tells us he saw us earlier in the day when his crew was hauling equipment to a new work site by truck. He said to a coworker, "Look at those two, I wonder where they are going and came from." Well, a few hours later he gets the scoop directly from us. Oscar is a nice man, great with directions, and we enjoy visiting with him.

About five miles after meeting Oscar, we are in Arizona! We have really enjoyed New Mexico, but are looking forward to exploring Arizona.

Peter

At the Arizona state line, we stop at the Chief Yellowhorse Trading Post (museum and gift shop). The approach to the trading post on its gravel driveway, after the big Chief Yellowhorse billboard on the left and a full-size bison cutout on the right, is like a scene out of an old western movie. Directly in front of us is a huge cliff of red and gray rock with a giant cave in the middle. There are four teepees on a ledge above the cave entrance and one inside the opening, along with a giant dream catcher. It is not hard to imagine ancient peoples taking shelter inside the mouth of the cave.

To the left of the cave is an old log cabin-style, one-story building with a big yellow sign that reads "Chief Yellowhorse Get Your Kicks." Inside, the owner tells us the trading post has been in his family for many years. It is an interesting place with lots of Native American artifacts, beautiful jewelry, rugs, beads, etc. The best part about the trading post, though, is that the main building straddles the New Mexico/Arizona state line, and the line is painted right on the floor.

Tracy

We tease the owner that he must have to pay taxes in two states. He laughs and says, "I think I pay taxes to everyone." The owner is the fourth generation of his family to run the trading post. I ask him who plans to take over when he is done, and he says he is not sure there is an interest from anyone in the next generation, and of course everyone has different ideas as to how the property should be used. Only, time will tell!

The Chief Yellowhorse Trading Post in Lupton, Arizona, sits at (make that "on") the border of New Mexico and Arizona.

Chief Yellowhorse Trading Post

"The Chief Yellowhorse Trading Post on Interstate 40 (Exit 359) is an interesting place to visit. The trading post, which is on the Navajo Reservation is located in two states, New Mexico and Arizona, a line painted on the floor of the trading post clearly shows the divide. The Yellowhorse family has been welcoming travelers since the 1950's when the family put up a roadside stand to sell Navajo rugs and petrified wood. Traveling Route 66 at that time was an adventure in itself with places to stop few and far between. The need to stop and stretch along with an interest to meet the Navajo family was the ingredient for success and great memories for everyone.

"The trading post was originally operated by Juan 'Chief' Yellowhorse, a Navajo Indian. He was born in 1930 and died in 1999. In 1960 he bought the Old Miller Trading Post and changed the name to the Chief Yellowhorse Trading Post. At that time Juan and Frank Yellowhorse expanded the roadside stand to a larger trading post and added gas pumps. New signs along Route 66 bought in more visitors."
https://www.theroute-66.com/

Peter

From the Trading Post, we head to the Arizona visitors center, one-half mile off route. While the restrooms are open, we are disappointed to discover that the visitor center has been permanently closed. Bummer! All that is left to do is take the obligatory photo by the "Arizona" sign and get back on the road. Done! With only thirty miles to go, it is time to suffer!

As predicted, a ridiculous 24-mph headwind has picked up, and Chambers and our hotel are on the other side of it. We shorten our normal pulls and breaks from fifteen miles to more manageable ten-mile segments. These are taking us about an hour to complete before we rest. You do the math.

The wind is so strong at one point we take refuge under an overpass.

Eventually, we reach Chambers, but not before making one last rest stop, only one mile away, and with our hotel in sight. We are pooped! We stop at the only gas station for a snack, and I slam a huge jug of chocolate milk and consider downing another. Feeling a bit better, we head to the hotel to see if it is open. It is, but check-in takes almost a half hour, even though we are the only ones at the counter. Luckily, we had a snack before we got here. According to the hotel desk clerk, the restaurant next door just reopened last week. Thank goodness.

Our last heroic effort for the day is to carry the tandem to our room on the second floor of the Days Inn. This always seems to happen when we are the most tired.

There is way less wind predicted for tomorrow, and we are excited because we will be riding and exploring Petrified Forest National Park.

Native American Fry Bread

Fry Bread batter is a four-ingredient bread that fries up crunchy and crispy on the outside while light, tasty, and tender on the inside. For dessert, sprinkle with brown sugar and cinnamon straight out of the fryer, or better yet, dust with powdered sugar, drizzle with honey, or for a savory dish, top with taco meat and fixings for Fry Bread Tacos.

Author: Beth Pierce
Prep Time: 20 minutes
Cook Time: 15 minutes
Total Time: 35 minutes plus resting time
Yield: 6

INGREDIENTS
2 cups all-purpose flour
2 1/2 teaspoons baking powder
1/2 teaspoon salt
1 cup warm water
vegetable oil for frying

INSTRUCTIONS
In a medium bowl, whisk flour, baking powder, and salt. Slowly stir in warm water with a fork. Mix just until the dough comes together. Use only as much water as you need for the dough to come together. Cover with wrap and let rest for 1 to 2 hours. Flour your hands and the working surface. Pull off a piece a little smaller than a golf ball. Roll into a ball, then pat it out to 1/8 to 1/4 inch thick.

In a heavy pan, heat 1-2 inches of oil to 375 degrees. Fry until the bread is golden brown and puffs up, about 2-3 minutes. Flip halfway through to brown the other side. Remove to paper towels to drain.

Tracy

The ride today was tough. I feel like I keep saying this, but again we had some strong headwinds and the heat to deal with. We heard from a local that the Santa Anna winds are typically strong this time of year and come from the west. Riding Route 66 from east to west may not have been the best idea due to the prevailing west winds. Oh well, we are almost done, so we will just keep heading west and deal with it.

We have dinner at the restaurant adjacent to the hotel and Peter orders a Navajo Taco, basically a taco on Indian fry bread. Our meals are delicious and filling.

Facebook followers

Richard C. Moeur (traffic engineer for the state of Arizona)
That wind can get mighty brutal. It may not be your best friend between there and Flagstaff. Glad to hear that Yellowhorse was open (when we'd go by, they'd be closed more often than not). Fun place, nice people. Only problem with staying in Chambers is if the restaurants are closed, the only dining option is the gas station. Don't know if the Apple Dumpling is still open (north of the freeway).

Re Holbrook: If you want to see if the Wigwam Motel still has rooms for tomorrow, call them at 928-524-3048 (they often book up every night in summer). If they're full, the Globetrotter Lodge across the street is excellent.

Will you be going through Petrified Forest on the park road, or direct to Holbrook?

Peter Flucke
The wind looks better tomorrow - fingers crossed! The restaurant in Chambers, next to the Days Inn, was open. I had a Navajo taco and it was great. We called the Wigwam a couple of days ago. They had a cancellation and we got in! We will be riding through Petrified Forest. Super excited!

Paul Knickelbine
Great but you look fat. Too many hash browns?

Greg Cribb
How long until you get to Flagstaff?

Peter Flucke
We plan to be there Thursday afternoon.

Greg Cribb
I will be in Flag on Friday.

Peter Flucke, July 11, 2016
It was a big jug of chocolate milk kind of day!

Dick Schaffer
What a great reward!

Elisa Pitrof
I think big is an understatement.

Lisa Reinke (physical therapist at Bellin Health, Green Bay, Wisconsin)
My favorite post-ride drink (well, other than beer).

The views from the overlooks along the Painted Desert were truly awe-inspiring.

Peter

(I now make Indian fry bread at home, and having Navajo tacos with our daughter and son-in-law in Green Bay has become an annual tradition.)

Day 40
July 12 – Chambers to Holbrook, Arizona
72 miles (total miles – 2,251)
Sunny, 89 degrees, 24 mph headwind for last 20 miles

Tracy

We are up early and on the road by 6:45 a.m. to hopefully beat the heat and wind a bit. We also want to spend as much time as possible in Petrified Forest National Park. The first twenty-three miles of our ride is on I-40/US Route 66. All but the last five miles to the park are downhill. Once in the park, we will travel twenty-eight miles on Petrified Forest Road from the north park entrance to the south entrance on Highway 180. The park road is the most beautiful ride you can imagine. It is in great shape, there are very few cars, and they are moving very slowly, but it is a bit hilly.

Our first stop is the visitor center, right at 8 a.m., to get a map, chat with a ranger, watch the informational movie, and figure out what we want to see. I also get my second flat penny of the trip. After a snack we are on our way to explore the park. We do drive-bys of several Painted Desert overlooks, but are still able to see the unbelievably beautiful colors weaving through the rocks. Our first stop is the Painted Desert Inn, a restored trading post, turned inn, turned museum, and National Historic Landmark.

We see a rusty old car in a vehicle pullout just north of the I-40 underpass and stop to check it out. The pullout showcases a section of old Route 66 that passed through the park. From the pullout, visitors can view the roadbed and telephone poles that mark the route of the famous "Main Street of America." The car is a relic 1932 Studebaker.

Puerco Pueblo is our first hiking stop. We walk the short trail to see some petroglyphs and the pueblo. It is very interesting and something I have never seen before. We stop and talk with a volunteer working at one of the buildings. She is so excited when she sees Peter's Green Bay Packers hat. She is a hardcore fan from Arizona.

Painted Desert Inn

"In its almost 100 years overlooking the Painted Desert, the inn has undergone many changes. The original building from the early 1920s was made of petrified wood. Today's adobe facade dates to the 1930s renovation of the Painted Desert Inn.

"The national historic landmark functions only as a museum now, with no overnight accommodation and food service. Displays inside highlight the building's history, Route 66, and the Civilian Conservation Corps. There are also restored murals by Hopi artist Fred Kabotie." https://www.nps.gov/pefo/learn/historyculture/pdi.htm

Our next stop is Crystal Forest, which is amazing. It is an area of the park that has thousands of pieces of petrified wood laying around. The petrified logs glimmer with quartz crystals as we walk along the short Crystal Forest trail.

Peter
As beautiful as the surrounding landscape is, we are glad the trail is short.

Petrified logs highlight the Crystal Forest trail in Petrified Forest National Park.

About Puerco Pueblo

"A series of droughts in the 1200s, during the Pueblo IV period, led ancestral Puebloan people to move away from small, scattered hamlets and instead build large pueblo communities. The Village on the Rio Puerco (or Puerco Pueblo, for short) is a 100+ room pueblo site located near the Puerco River, a major drainage that bisects the park. The river would have been a reliable source of water for crops. Farming of corn, beans, and squash took place on the floodplains and terraces along the river. The river also made a natural travel corridor, meaning travelers and traders frequented Puerco Pueblo, carrying new ideas as well as goods.

"At its largest size, around 1300, Puerco Pueblo may have been home to about 200 people. The one-story high village of hand-shaped sandstone blocks was built around a rectangular plaza. The rooms were living quarters and storage, but most activity, like cooking and craft making, took place in the plaza. There were also several underground rooms, called kivas, where ceremonial practices took place. There were no doors or windows in the plaster-covered exterior walls of the pueblo. Entry into the village was by ladders over the wall and across the log, brush, and mud roofs of the room blocks.

"Unable to adapt to the climate change of the late 1300s, the inhabitants of Puerco Pueblo systematically abandoned the pueblo in search of a more suitable area. It was all but empty by 1380. Only the sandstone bricks, potsherds, stone tools, petroglyphs, and other artifacts and features remain to tell the tale of these ancient people."

https://www.nps.gov/pefo/learn/historyculture/puerco-pueblo.htm

There is virtually no shade here, or anywhere else in the park for that matter, and the increasing wind with only seven percent humidity makes it feel like we are walking through a blast furnace.

Tracy

Our final stop is the Rainbow Forest Museum and south visitor center. We take a short break sitting on a nicely shaded bench near the museum. Our bicycle is leaning against the back of the bench because there are no bike racks available. Two young women and a young man from Arizona stop to ask about our trip. They are very interested and ask lots of questions. We enjoy talking with them for about a half hour and learn more about Arizona. We give them a business card and suggest they check out our social media and ask them to send us a message. They say they will.

We finally lock the bicycle to the bench and wander over to the visitor center to fill our water bottles and hit the bathroom before we leave. The Giant Logs Trail is located here. We do not hike it because of the heat, but we get a good view from the back deck. Upon our return to the bicycle, there are four older women sitting on "our bicycle rack" bench, and we talk with them about our trip. They are also traveling Route 66, but by car, and are obviously having a great time exploring together. They are formidable women and would

Rainbow Forest Museum

"Rainbow Forest was the heart of the original Petrified Forest set aside by President Roosevelt as a national monument in 1906. One of the earliest facilities in the park was a wood and tar paper shack near where the current museum is located." https://www.nps.gov/pefo/learn/historyculture/rainbow-forest-museum.htm

"Giant Logs Trail features some of the largest and most colorful logs in the park. 'Old Faithful,' at the top of the trail, is almost ten feet wide at the base!" https://www.nps.gov/places/giant-logs-trail.htm

fit right in with the Red Hat Society.

We politely ask them to get up so we can remove our bicycle. They stand right up and say they certainly do not want to delay our trip. We talk a bit more and then head toward Holbrook on Highway 180. "Only" twenty miles to go.

The ride to Holbrook is tough. The westerly headwind has kicked up to 24 mph, and it is hot, 89 degrees. No fun at all. We cannot even talk to distract each other from our misery because of the wind noise. At least we are going downhill primarily. About halfway through the ride, as we both are in an "I am so done with this" mood, we experience a much-needed random act of kindness.

We have our heads down and are pounding on the pedals when I happen to look to my left and see a small SUV traveling next to us with a woman holding two ice-cold bottles of water out the passenger window. She is trying to ask if we want them.

I yell over the wind to Peter, "Do you want water?"

"What?"

"DO YOU WANT WATER!?"

"No! I don't want water. I have water, same as you, and it is over 100 degrees!"

Just then, Peter sees the SUV, the woman, and the two bottles of water. Ugh! Completely chagrinned, he, gently, yells back, "Yes, please."

We pull over to the side of the road and the woman, with her husband, and two small children in the back seat, hands us the two sweating bottles of water. We pour the scalding water out of our water bottles and refill them from theirs. We thank the family, and off they go. What a wonderful thing for them to do. The last ten miles to Holbrook fly by.

We make it to Holbrook (pop. 5,026) about forty-five minutes later and get settled in our home for the night, wigwam 16 at the Wigwam Village Motel #6. This is not our first experience staying in a wigwam. Several years ago, we stayed at Wigwam Village Motel #2 in Cave City, Kentucky, while on vacation with our girls to see Mammoth Cave. We are excited to stay in one again and it brings back fond memories.

While chilling in the wigwam, my phone rings. It is my older brother Bill calling from Milwaukee.

The Wigwam Village Motel #6 was our home for the night in Holbrook, Arizona, as we contemplated the wisdom of bicycling across the Mojave Desert ahead.

Wigwam Village Motel #6 in Holbrook, Arizona

"While passing through Cave City, Kentucky, in 1938, Chester E. Lewis was impressed by the distinctive design of the original Wigwam Village constructed in 1937 by architect Frank Redford. An astute observer will see that the Wigwam Village is not composed of wigwams but of teepees. Mr. Redford, who patented the wigwam village design in 1936, disliked the word 'teepee' and ignoring cultural accuracy used 'wigwam' instead.

"Mr. Lewis purchased copies of the plans and the right to use the Wigwam Village name. The purchase included a royalty agreement in which Mr. Lewis would install coin operated radios, and every dime inserted for 30 minutes of play would be sent to Mr. Redford as payment. Seven Wigwam Villages were constructed between 1936 and the 1950s. Finished in 1950, Mr. Lewis' village was the sixth, thus its designation as Wigwam Village #6.

"Mr. Lewis successfully operated the motel until I-40 bypassed downtown Holbrook in the late 1970s. Mr. Lewis sold the business, and two years after his death, his wife and grown children re-purchased the property and reopened the motel in 1988." https://www.nps.gov/places/wigwam-village-motel-6.htm

"Burrrhead" (Bill's childhood nickname for me), how are you and Petey doing? I have been following your posts. You guys are cruising right along and getting close to the Mojave Desert. What are your plans for crossing the desert?"

"We have been thinking about that," I reply. "For now, we plan to take it one day at a time and get some local intel as we get closer."

"You know Pat (Kolp) and I just got back from our motorcycle trip and crossed the Mojave; it was hotter than hell and we really struggled. I don't know how you two idiots are going to bicycle across! Please think about this, I am worried about you!"

"We will. Love you Bill."

"Love you, too."

Day 41
July 13 – Holbrook to Winslow, Arizona
39 miles (total miles – 2,290)
Sunny, low 80s early in day, 100 degrees by noon,
slight tailwind early to headwind after noon

Tracy

We wake up in our wigwam early to get our miles done before the temperature and wind all rise!

Peter

Today is a short day because it is about thirty-nine miles from Holbrook to Winslow, and another sixty-one miles, uphill, with no services, from Winslow to Flagstaff. One hundred miles from Holbrook to Flagstaff just isn't going to happen.

Tracy

We are on the road by 7 a.m. The first twenty miles are on smaller county roads to Joseph City.

As we are taking a break along the side of the road, a car approaches us going really slowly. We are wondering what is up, and then they pull alongside us. It is the four women we met at Petrified Forest National Park yesterday. They are taking a side trip to see a cool bridge they heard about. It is fun to see them again and they tell us they saw us heading out of Holbrook this morning while eating breakfast at a local restaurant. This time, we give them our card and tell them to follow our trip and send us messages. They say they will.

Joseph City is supposed to have a convenience store and restaurant, but not anymore. Luckily, a local volunteer firefighter has just arrived at the fire station we are bicycling past and is kind enough to fill our water bottles for us. He tells us the local power plant is closing and many people in town have lost their jobs. Businesses have closed because the people are gone.

Peter

From Joseph City, we ride on the I-40 frontage road. The road is in bad shape, one of the worst we have ridden on this trip, and it is bouncing us all over the place.

All about jackrabbits

"The black-tailed jackrabbit and antelope jackrabbit are often seen idling or running together in Arizona and Mexico, where their ranges overlap. But make no mistake—these are two different species. Even small traits count. Both hares have long ears and legs, but antelope jackrabbits' ears are even more enormous. Black-tailed jackrabbits are distinguished by black tails and ear-tips. In a race, the antelope jackrabbit would win, reaching speeds of 44 miles (72 kilometers) per hour."
https://www.amnh.org/exhibitions/permanent/north-american-mammals/black-tailed-and-antelope-jackrabbits

Eventually, we are forced to slow down to avoid losing our bags or damaging the bike. Humorously, we are not the only things bouncing around out here. There are jackrabbits everywhere. Our slower pace allows us to appreciate how they have adapted to this harsh environment and their athleticism. Damn, those things are fast.

Tracy

The good thing about being on the frontage road is that we finally get to visit the Jack Rabbit Trading Post. The trading post has been in existence for more than sixty-six years. Its claim to fame is its jackrabbit logo, which was once plastered all over Route 66. Think North Dakota's Wall Drug signs. We have been seeing Jack Rabbit Trading Post signs for miles and miles. As we pedal toward the trading post, we see a gentleman standing on the side of the road videotaping us. Kind of strange. So, of course, we stop to chat. He is from Indiana and is in Arizona with a church youth group to do volunteer work at a local Native American group home. He is also a bicyclist and has lots of questions for us, which we dutifully answer.

We get back on I-40 and follow it for seventeen miles into Winslow (pop. 9,608). We arrive by 11 a.m., nice and early. We totally beat the heat and wind for once. We can get into our hotel room at La Posada Hotel, Restaurant, Museum, and Gardens right away.

We had been seeing signs for the Jack Rabbit Trading Post for many miles. This one tells us we had officially arrived.

La Posada was designed by Mary Colter (1869-1958), an American architect and designer. One of a very few female American architects in her day, Colter designed many landmark buildings and spaces for the Fred Harvey Company and the Santa Fe Railroad, notably in nearby Grand Canyon National Park.

Famous hotel guests include Albert Einstein, Amelia Earhart, Franklin Delano Roosevelt, Betty Grable, and John Wayne.

The timing of the opening of this amazing building could not have been worse. The year 1930 was right at the start of the Great Depression. The building never prospered and closed to the public in 1957. The property was gutted in 1961 and transformed into offices for the Santa Fe Railroad. (The tracks are right behind the building, and it also serves as an Amtrak Depot). The railroad was going to dispose of La Posada in 1993, but luckily, the National Trust for Historic Preservation put the property on its endangered list in 1994. Ultimately, Allan Affeldt purchased the property from the Santa Fe Railroad and renovated it. This is an amazing property and has several unique hotel rooms named after famous people.

We are staying in the Franklin Delano Roosevelt room. If you are ever in Winslow, Arizona, definitely check it out. Better yet, spend the night.

After we get settled in, of course we have to stop at the famous corner in Winslow dedicated to the Eagles' hit song *Take It Easy*. The corner has a bronze statue of a man leaning against a lamp post with a guitar in his hand with the words "Standing on the Corner" on a sign above his head. On a windowsill in the background is a stuffed eagle and a picture of a blonde in a red flatbed Ford truck. If you have not heard the song, it is a good one and they say it helped put Winslow, Arizona, on the map.

Day 42
July 14 – Winslow to Flagstaff, Arizona
63 miles (total miles – 2,353)
Sunny, 85 degrees, slight headwind

Tracy

We are up at 4:30 a.m., eager to get an early start on the day. "Breakfast" (coffee and tea) is available in the lobby at 5 a.m. and sunrise is at 5:09 a.m. I bring drinks back to the room to enjoy with our own instant oatmeal and dried fruit.

We are on the bicycle and heading out of Winslow by 6 a.m. Just two miles into the ride, our route has us back on I-40 for thirty-nine miles.

Peter

The heat and wind are going to increase about noon, and we have a climb of over 2,000 feet to Flagstaff. Thank goodness the bulk of our ride is on I-40, so the uphill is pretty gentle. The only bad parts are all the traffic noise

We had to take our turn posing with the statue at the iconic spot in Winslow, Arizona, made famous by the Eagles' hit song "Take it Easy." Notice the "girl, my Lord, in a flatbed Ford" behind us.

Elisa Pitrof
Please tell me you have heard "Route 66" by Manhattan Transfer...ear worm... UGH!

Darlene Luedtke Charles
Such a Fine Sight to See ...

Thomas Florack (friend, orthopedic surgeon, and home brewer)
I see the girl, but no flatbed Ford...

Peter Flucke
Oh, Tom. Look at the window behind me.

Thomas Florack
Too fun!

and lots of asphalt to look at. We climb steadily for the first nineteen miles to a freeway rest stop. After that, we go to ten-mile pulls, followed by a short break, to accommodate our tired bodies (this is day six on the bike), the altitude (5,000-6,000 feet, plus) and my slight headache.

We get off the interstate at the city of Winona and begin our final twenty-mile climb to Flagstaff. The back roads allow us to enjoy the emerging forest and the mountains in peace and quiet. The climb is not too bad, but definitely steeper than the climb on the interstate. We are now bicycling on Townsend-Winona Road/Old Route 66 and luckily, a huge section of the road was just repaved. It is a pleasure to ride on, we have a nice clean, wide, shoulder all to ourselves.

Tracy

We reach the outskirts of Flagstaff (pop. 71,254) and our map directs us to Highway 89 for eight miles to the historic downtown. The map addendum tells me Highway 89 is not fun to ride. It has way too much traffic and no bicycle facilities. Great, now we have traffic! Highway 89 is five lanes wide and packed. At least there is a bike lane, a tiny one, but we have some space. Eventually, we have had enough of the traffic and are starting to bonk, so we stop at a Starbucks for a pick-me-up. Thank goodness for coffee. Checking the GPS, we discover we are only 1.4 miles away from historic downtown Flagstaff. We made it!

Peter

We are staying at a hostel tonight, Motel Du Beau. The motel is old school, with tiny rooms (the tandem just fits) and no AC, but it is very clean, comfortable, and you cannot beat the location. It is right in the middle of the downtown area and within walking distance of just about everything we need. There are even three microbreweries close by. I am in heaven.

After getting settled, we walk .1 miles to a bike shop for supplies, then next door to Mother Road Brewing Company for a beer. Later, I walk .3 miles to get my hair cut. For dinner, we walk another .3 miles to Lumber Yard Brewing Company. Finally, we walk .3 miles to get coffee and then .1 miles back to the motel. We are exhausted from all the walking.

We are taking the day off tomorrow and our friend Greg, who lives in Phoenix, will be picking us up in the morning. Greg used to work at our local bike shop, JB Cycle & Sport, and we rode together often. Greg is an amazing cyclist and routinely kicked my butt. He will be our tour guide for the day. It sounds like he is taking us hiking and then out to lunch. It will be great to see him as it has been years. We are looking forward to a day off the bicycle and a chance to catch up with an old friend.

Facebook followers

Peter Flucke, July 14, 2016
44 miles and 1,500 feet of climbing in since Winslow, Arizona. Starting to feel it on my knees and lungs. 20 miles and 700 feet left to go to Flagstaff!

Darlene Luedtke Charles
Please don't tell me you two have to ride all the way back to Green Bay once you get to your destination?

Peter Flucke
Nope! Amtrak (Los Angeles - Milwaukee)

Darlene Luedtke Charles
THANK GOD! My butt's getting sore just trying to keep up to you two.

Dawn N Hal Goodman
You two are amazing. Ride On!

Lynn Young Tulachka
You still have a smile. You're amazing.

Marty Zeske
Totally awesome!

Paula Roberts
Maybe you'll have some cooler weather in Flagstaff! Good luck and have fun!

Thomas Florack
Go Team!

Shelley Barstow
Wonderful! I bet you'll be ready for yoga when you return.

Collette LaRue
Wow! Go Peter and Tracy!

Ann Evans Dettlaff
You're holding up remarkably well for an old guy! Keep it up. I'm incredibly impressed with your progress.

Shelley Barstow
U r such a good team with your strength, energy, and persistence.

We usually stayed active even on our days off the bike. Here we are at the end of the Cathedral Rock Trail in Sedona, Arizona.

Day 43
July 15 – Flagstaff, Arizona
0 miles (total miles – 2,353)
Sunny, 90 degrees, slight headwind

Tracy

Today is a day off the bike. Our friend Greg was already planning to be in Flagstaff for a long weekend of hiking with friends, and he offered to show us the area. We happily accepted. Greg arrives at our motel at 9 a.m. and we are off in his car for a day of fun and adventure. We start with a one-hour drive south to Sedona to hike/climb Cathedral Rock Trail, one of the Red Rock Trails in the Coconino National Forest. The views are simply stunning!

After the climb, we hike down to Oak Creek, which flows through the canyon near the trail, and play in the swimming hole. The cold water feels great and we can see the climb we made from the creek. Next, we head to a small winery (Page Springs Cellars) for lunch. Generally beer people, we enjoy broadening our horizons with some vino. Both the food and the wine are wonderful. We soak in the scenery as much as possible on our way back to Flagstaff and all enjoy a short nap at the motel.

At 6:30 p.m., we walk to Flagstaff Brewing Company to meet two of Greg's backpacking friends (Phillip and Danielle) for dinner, and of course a beer. We pick up our third Flagstaff brewery glass. Now we must figure out how to fit them all on the bike and find a post office in our next stop in Williams, Arizona. It's too late to find an open post office here in Flagstaff. Beer glasses are really a dumb thing to collect on a cross-country bicycle trip. My flat penny collection is looking better and better.

We thoroughly enjoy our evening. It is fun to meet some of Greg's friends and learn more about them and Flagstaff.

After dinner, I head to the motel to call my brother, Bill. He has texted me a couple of times today to check on our progress.

"So, what are your plans for crossing the Mojave Desert?" Bill asks.

"We have been talking with locals and the majority advise us to drive across the desert," I reply. "It's just too hot this time of year to safely bicycle. We are planning to reach out to car rental companies tomorrow. We will try to rent a car from a city as far west as possible."

"Oh, thank goodness! Now I don't have to hire the water truck to follow you across the desert. Keep me posted, let me know if you need anything, and enjoy your trip."

"I will. Thanks much. Love you."

Peter goes out with the rest of the gang for "just one more." He is back by 10 p.m.

This picture removes all doubt that we have the ability to expand our boundaries beyond craft beer and appreciate a bottle of fine wine as well.

Facebook followers

Peter Flucke is with Tracy Flucke at Page Springs Cellars
July 15, 2016, Cornville, AZ
A little something different for us. Thanks Greg Cribb!

Ann Evans Dettlaff
What? Wine?? You finally have arrived.

Elisa Pitrof
Now you're talking my language!

Facebook followers

Paul Knickelbine
The rest is all downhill - put the Santa Annas to work.

Rebecca Cleveland
Cathedral Rock! Very cool hike, and fun mountain biking on the slickrock face.

Peter Flucke
Very true, but we decided not to give it a try with the tandem. Lol

Noralyn Smiley
Sedona is a beautiful place. Glad you got to see it.

Day 44
July 16 – Flagstaff to Williams, Arizona
33 miles (total miles – 2,386)
Sunny, 90 degrees, slight headwind

Peter

We are in no big hurry to get going this morning with only thirty something miles to go to Williams. All we need to do is pack, eat breakfast, and change a soft front tire. Once again, a small piece of wire, probably from another failed truck tire along I-40, was stuck in the tire and had penetrated the tube, ever so slightly. It is an easy change and way more enjoyable to complete in the motel room than along the freeway.

We are on the road by 8 a.m. and heading uphill out of town toward I-40. Not fun when you are at altitude and not warmed up yet. The ride is mostly downhill once on the interstate. That's nice, but the shoulder is deteriorated worse than most we have been on so far. It is cracked, covered with gravel, and littered with tire pieces. We are glad it is a short ride today.

Nineteen miles into the ride, we stop at a small gas station/post office/convenience store in the village of Parks for a snack and to fill our water bottles. There is a Little Free Library in the gas station, and Tracy is excited because she needs a new book and finds a good one.

Leaving Parks, we ride on Old Route 66, which has recently been repaved. The road is as smooth as silk and has a nice, wide shoulder. This part of the ride is through a heavily wooded area. It is nice to see trees again, and we really enjoy the shade and wind block!

We arrive in Williams around 11 a.m. Since the Grand Canyon Hotel, where we are staying for the night, does not open until 2 p.m., we decide to eat a second breakfast and explore town. With full stomachs, Tracy wanders around town and checks out all the shops while I sit on a bench near the hotel and watch the world go by. We both enjoy the afternoon.

We check into the hotel at 2 p.m. Built in 1891, it is a great old property, modernized enough, but not too much.

Later, while I get caught up on social media, Tracy picks up our tickets for the Grand Canyon Railway. We are taking the train to the south rim of the Canyon tomorrow. Neither of us has been to Grand Canyon National Park. We are excited to see it.

We spend the rest of the afternoon working on logistics for the end of the trip and napping.

The Grand Canyon Hotel

"The Grand Canyon Hotel opened its doors in January 1891 and is the oldest hotel in Arizona. Williams was a logging, ranching, mining, and fur-trapping town. In 1905, the Santa Fe railroad opened a spur up to the Grand Canyon, making Williams 'The Gateway to the Grand Canyon.' The Grand Canyon Hotel was the only hotel close to the Grand Canyon at the time.

"It is a European-style hotel... ... (In) the guest registers from 1904 ... are such famous guests as General Pershing (who was a captain at the time) and the Vanderbilts. The King of Siam and John Muir (founder of the Sierra Club) stayed here 4 times. Other guests from the 1940s and '50s reveal the rooms were rented more than once the same night (Ummm).

"The hotel closed about 1970 after Interstate 40 bypassed Williams and sat empty for 35 years. New owners purchased the hotel in 2004 and started the complete remodel, re-opening for business in June of 2005, including all new electricity and plumbing.

"The Grand Canyon Hotel is located in the center of Williams at the crossroads of Route 66 and Second Street." https://thegrandcanyonhotel.com/history/

Tracy

Someone is napping, but not me. I am trying to rent a car to drive across the Mojave Desert, and it is proving to be difficult. In fact, after two hours I am beginning to think it is not possible. I have spoken to car rental agencies as far west as Kingman (130 miles from Williams) and no cars are available. We aren't even picky; any size car will work because the tandem has S&S couplers which allow us to break it down into small pieces (think large-size suitcase). I finally decide I need a break and we head out to do laundry and explore town some more. Not being able to find a car rental is still weighing on me. How the heck are we going to get across the desert safely?

Peter

With our chores done for the day, we walk a couple of blocks to the Grand Canyon Brewing Company. We each have a beer and polish off a small bucket of salted peanuts. I guess we were hungry. Of course, we pick up another beer glass. We return to the hotel, where Tracy packs our (now) four beer glasses in a box we scrounged from the front desk clerk. We will take them to the post office tomorrow morning. We have dinner at a Thai restaurant right behind our hotel and turn in early.

Peter Flucke is at the Grand Canyon Brewing Company.

Richard C. Moeur
Toasting tomorrow's plummet? Don't forget the pie at Pine Country Restaurant. When you get to Seligman, don't forget to stop at Angel & Vilma Delgadillo's Original Route 66 Gift Shop. And Delgadillo's Snow Cap Burger Stand too.

Peter Flucke
Thanks! Won't be tomorrow though. We are taking the train to the south rim of the Canyon.

Mike Gerke
One glass a night. 4 months on road. You'll need to build some new bar glass cabinets.

Peter Flucke
Right!

Who are we kidding with drinking wine? Time to get back to our craft beer roots.

Day 45
July 17 – Williams, Arizona
0 miles (total miles – 2,386)
Beautiful, 85 degrees, partly cloudy

Tracy

Since we are not bicycling today and the train to the Grand Canyon does not board until 9:15 a.m., we take our time getting going. I am tempted to work on our car rental problem, but decide to relax instead so I can enjoy the day. The problem will still be there when we get back. Somehow, things will work out. They always do.

We stop at the post office after breakfast at a local restaurant to mail our pint glasses home, and then wander over to the train station to watch the wild west show. The show, featuring the "Cataract Gang," is definitely G-rated, but it is still kind of fun. It is even more fun, though, to watch the kids in the audience. They are wired.

Our train leaves at 9:30 a.m. sharp. We are riding in a meticulously restored 1920s Pullman car. Trains are always fun for Peter because his maternal grandfather, Robert Wiechmann, worked for the Southern Pacific Railroad out of San Francisco for forty-two years. Trains are in his blood. Peter says his grandpa could tell how fast a train was going by counting how many times the train car wheels went clickity clack on the rail joints in one minute. It isn't hard to imagine we are making the trip to the canyon in a bygone era. We arrive at the south rim two and half hours later.

The Grand Canyon is incredible. The scale is so immense that it takes us awhile to feel comfortable. One mile almost straight down to the Colorado River is a long way down. We walk along the canyon edge and even venture down into the canyon a bit on Bright Angel Trail. We most definitely need to come back and hike to the bottom of the canyon someday. (Our daughter, Melissa, and son-in-law, Dillon (the cheese guy), completed the one-day, twenty-five-mile Grand Canyon rim-to-rim hike in 2022. They ended their hike on the south rim on the Bright Angel Trail.)

Peter

We have about three hours to explore the park, which is really just enough time to get an overview of this amazing place. The National Park Service has done an incredible job of managing the south rim. It is easy to get around and safe, yet we do not feel like we are restricted in our movements. We really get to experience the canyon; well, at least the south rim.

The Grand Canyon, while stunningly beautiful, is no joke. This hot, arid, high-altitude environment is fraught with danger for the uninformed, cavalier, or over-confident traveler. A poster we see tacked to a post near the Bright Angel Trail states: "What Goes Down, Must Come Back Up." Under the heading "Tips For All Hikers," it lists: Double your Food Intake; Drink LOTS of Fluids; Wait for Shade or Cooler Temperatures; Stay Wet and Stay

We enjoyed our short visit to the South Rim of the Grand Canyon. We will have to come back someday with more time to explore.

Cool; Regulate your Pace; and Rest Often.

Then they get serious with the heading, "Special Note to the Young, Strong, and Invincible: Let's take a short quiz before hiking into the abyss.

1) At what temperature will your brain FRY (and you die) from extreme heat exposure and dehydration leaving you utterly useless? Answer: When your core body temperature reaches 105 degrees or greater. (This can happen at any summer temperature when you're overheated and under-fueled.)

2), Etc."

To hammer home the point, the poster ends with: "NO KIDDING – DO NOT attempt to hike from the rim to the river and back without being prepared to possibly suffer the following: Permanent brain damage; Cardiac arrest; Death!"

A bit later, we encounter a much larger sign that features the word "WARNING" and a picture of a fit-looking, middle-aged man on all fours puking his guts out. This environment is no joke!

We need to make our way back to the train all too soon for the ride back to Williams. The ride is uneventful, except for a staged train robbery by the Cataract Gang.

Back in Williams, I check the weather in Needles, California, 180 miles to our west on Route 66, in a last-ditch attempt to find a way to make the desert bikeable. Nope, it's not! The temperature is currently 108 degrees in Needles with a 26-mph wind out of the southeast and gusts to 35 mph. Even if we load ourselves down with all the water and Gatorade we can carry, I cannot guarantee we will be able to make it to our first water stop, let alone a second should the first stop turn out to be a mirage. Live to ride another day. We need to find a rental car!

We wander over to the grocery store to pick up supplies, and something for dinner and breakfast tomorrow morning.

"So, what are we going to do about the desert?" I ask Tracy on our stroll back to the hotel. "This is more than just a risk; I don't even think it is possible right now. Remember, the one thing we cannot do is die."

(I am thankful this is our third major cross-country bicycle trip and not our first. My desire to complete our first trip across the Northern Tier end to end under our own power came close to creating an unacceptable risk once or twice. Think near hypothermia in a thunderstorm, then turning down a ride into town and taking an open-air ferry across Lake Champlain between New York and Vermont in a different thunderstorm. And I hate lightning. See our book *Coast to Coast on a Tandem*.)

"I don't know," Tracy replies sadly. Just then, I happen to look up and I start to laugh.

"What?" Tracy says.

I smile and just point up. Tracy starts to laugh too. Almost directly over our heads is a large black and orange sign that reads, "U-Haul."

Tracy

As we are walking back to our hotel, Peter says, "That guy in the crosswalk looks just like Randy Johnson."

I say, "That is Randy, and Julie, and their granddaughter."

The Johnsons are our neighbors from Green Bay, two doors down. What a small world. It is so great to see them and talk for a while. They are on a two-week vacation and traveling across the United States as well. They had been following us on Facebook, but were surprised to see us because they thought we were in Las Vegas, Nevada, as opposed to Las Vegas, New Mexico. Peter and I

Facebook followers

Peter Flucke is with Tracy Flucke at South Rim of the Grand Canyon.

Having a Grand time!

John Z Wetmore
It looks like Arizona has an erosion problem.

Patrick Kolp
Yep, looks the same as it did 5 weeks ago, stay safe.

Ann Evans Dettlaff
Cool picture of you two.

Ruth Flucke
What a great photo - an awesome couple in an awesome place. Love yous 100%.

Evan Gore (Peter's high school friend)
I don't say this lightly or easily, but what you two do is... amazing.

Peter Flucke
Thanks Evan!

Collette LaRue
Ahhh the GC!

Thomas Florack
OHHH what a great view and OOOO what a bad pun!

Chinese bicycle tourist we met at our Warmshowers stay in Springfield, Illinois
Congratulations! Memorable place!

have been feeling a bit lonely lately and it is so nice to see someone from home!

After dinner at our hotel, we go out for one last beer and then call it a night.

Tomorrow, we will bicycle to Grand Canyon Caverns, a campground near Peach Springs. We will be heading downhill again the whole day. Yea! Thank you for the great visit, Williams.

> **Sheila Flucke (our sister-in-law)**
> Thanks, your pictures are getting me fired up! Only 2 more weeks and I'll be rafting and camping along that river. Can't wait to see the view from the bottom of the canyon!

Day 46
July 18 – Williams to Peach Springs, Arizona
69 miles (total miles – 2,455)
Partly cloudy, 80 degrees, soaking rain late in day

Tracy

We have a few things to take care of this morning before we hop on the bicycle. After figuring out last night that a U-Haul truck may be a possibility for getting us across the Mojave Desert, I am excited to see what I can find. I have determined that Kingman, Arizona, is the closest we can get to the desert and, hopefully, still find a U-Haul to rent. Success! My first call results in the rental of a ten-foot U-Haul truck from Kingman to San Bernardino, California.

This takes a huge weight off our shoulders. After talking with locals, my brother, checking the weather forecast, and reviewing Bob Robinson's book, *Bicycling Guide to Route 66*, we know driving across the desert rather than riding is the right choice for us. We have been using Bob's book as a supplement to the Adventure Cycling maps. In the section from Kingman, Arizona, to Goffs, California, the author warns riders, "Be sure to top off your water bottles at every opportunity, because services are limited through the early portion of the section and you are riding on the outskirts of the Mojave Desert, which often reports the highest recorded temperatures in the nation."

Peter

We finally get on the bicycle at about 9 a.m. and start our sixty-nine mile, mostly downhill, ride to the Grand Canyon Caverns/RV Park near Peach Springs. We get back on I-40 just outside of Williams and start a thirteen-mile run to Ash Forks. It is a great ride with beautiful views. Dropping from an elevation of 7,000 to 5,000 feet, we average 30 mph. We are flying. It only takes us forty minutes to reach Ash Forks.

Outside of Ash Forks, we get off the interstate and back onto Route 66. Evidently, this section of Route 66 is the longest continuous piece through

Tracy works on the logistics of renting a U-Haul truck to transport us and our tandem across the Mojave Desert while we relax in the Grand Canyon Hotel in Williams, Arizona.

the whole corridor. It is a nice ride with lots to see, including the rain clouds starting to surround us. Luckily, the rain holds off for quite a while, but after a short break in Seligman, it starts. The rain feels good, though, as it is getting a bit warm again.

Unfortunately, the rain starts to come down in buckets about ten miles down the road. We get soaked! We still have seven miles to go to the Grand Canyon Caverns/RV Park. Cold and wet, we finally arrive at the convenience store located just outside of the hotel/campground complex. Inside and out of the rain, we try to warm up and decide if we should bicycle the additional one mile to the campground or stay at the Caverns Hotel. We decide on the hotel because we are still soaked and I am feeling a bit under the weather, so to speak. This is a good choice and allows us to warm up and take care of some remaining logistics.

Tracy

We have been hearing about the "monsoon season" from the locals for several days. They tell us we are lucky we have not experienced a monsoon rainstorm and how intense they can be. Now we know; it is like going through a carwash without a car! At one point, I expected Peter to pull over because the water was getting so deep on the road my pedals were rotating through it. But we continued and a short time later the rain became a little less intense, making it possible for us to push on.

This ominous sign, which reads "300 Miles Desert Ahead," greeted us at the Hackberry General Store. It served as reinforcement of our decision to rent a U-Haul for the trek across the Mojave Desert.

Day 47
July 19 – Peach Springs to Kingman, Arizona
59 miles (total miles – 2,514)
Partly sunny, 65 degrees in the morning to 95 degrees late morning,
slight headwind

Kingman, Arizona, to San Bernardino, California
Traveled by U-Haul truck – 277 miles
110 degrees in Needles, California, with a 20-mph headwind

Tracy

We get up really early, 4:15 a.m., have breakfast, and are on the road by 6 a.m. We want to beat as much of the heat and wind as possible. We also want to give ourselves a buffer in case we have any problems. We need to pick up our U-Haul truck for the 275-mile desert crossing to San Bernardino, California, by 2 p.m.

Most of the ride is downhill and, mercifully, the wind is coming from behind us early. Twenty-four miles into the ride, we stop at an interesting convenience store in Hackberry. The store has tons of Route 66 memorabilia, and it is fun to check it all out. There is a very friendly cat at the store that I enjoy playing with, but it makes me miss our two kitties at home.

Peter

Just to the left of the Hackberry General Store, in a bed of cactus, is a large, rusted yellow sign with faded black letters that reads, "300 MILES DESERT AHEAD."

Okay!

After our stop, we cruise right along and get to Kingman, twenty-eight miles away, by 11 a.m.

Tracy

As we reach the near edge of Kingman, we see a touring bicyclist ahead of us and eventually catch up to him. He is from Germany and started his trip in New York City on April 1. He is heading to Las Vegas, Nevada, and then up to San Francisco. He tells us he is having fun, but getting sick of the constant headwinds. We agree, wish him luck, and continue on our way.

We make really good time and arrive at the U-Haul dealer a full three hours early. Our only issue on the ride this morning was a stiff headwind for the last ten miles. We will definitely not miss bicycling into the headwinds.

Peter

Surprisingly, the U-Haul rental facility already has a truck ready for us despite our early arrival. We change clothes in their bathroom and then unload the bicycle. Next, we hoist the tandem into the cavernous back of the truck. There is plenty of room – even to the point of overkill – and we rest the tandem gently against one wall. I use the paracord from our emergency kit and the truck's tiedowns to secure the bike to the wall. After pulling and tugging the bike in every direction I can think of, I deem it secure. We move a few essentials from our panniers into a small bag to take with us in the cab

We had to be careful securing our tandem and gear inside the larger-than-we-needed U-Haul truck. Better too spacious than too small, however.

Tracy pets one of the friendly cats that came to say hi outside of the Hackberry General Store.

Hackberry General Store, Mohave County

"Generously described as 'ramshackle,' Hackberry General Store has enthralled Route 66 pilgrims since Bob Waldmire reopened it in 1992. (Bob was a legendary Route 66er whose father invented the hot-dog-on-a-stick). The store, built in 1934, had been abandoned for 14 years, and Bob kept it looking that way. When Bob sold it to John Pritchard in 1998, it was with the understanding that John would maintain the store's dilapidated charm, and when John sold it to Amy Franklin in 2016, she agreed to do likewise.

"Hackberry General Store, apparently held together by the rusting signs nailed to its exterior, is the only outpost of civilization for miles. Its gas pumps have been dry for decades, but it still has a real, working outdoor pay phone because there's no mobile service in Hackberry. Visitors, many from countries other than the U.S., crowd into the store to soak in the crumbly Mother Road vibe, tack their paper money and patches to the walls, and buy Hackberry General Store snacks, t-shirts, and refrigerator magnets.

"A little of this 'real' Route 66 goes a long way, and it's reasonable to assume that if the Mother Road were still lined with Hackberry-like places, this one wouldn't seem so charming." https://www.roadsideamerica.com/story/23659

of the truck, tie down the remaining four bags in the back, and pull down and secure the overhead door. I offer to let Tracy drive (knowing there is no way in hell she is going to). She graciously declines. We orient ourselves to the truck, fill it with gas, grab some lunch, and then take off toward California.

The Mojave Desert is hot, windy, desolate, and beautiful. It is 110 degrees when we pass through Needles, California, and there is a 20-mph headwind. Services are as much as fifty-five miles apart. The route itself would have been difficult enough, but in one section we would have been on a very busy I-15 that was under construction and with no accommodations for bicyclists to get through safely. The temperature does not drop below 100 degrees all the way across the desert. The U-Haul's air conditioning can barely keep up. The floor of the truck is so hot we must constantly shift our feet to keep them from burning. We made a good choice driving!

Tracy

We make it to the Super 8 in San Bernardino, California, about 5:30 p.m. We are hot, tired, hungry, and stinky. Not a good combination. It has been a really long day. While unloading needed supplies for the night, I grab the small bag which has been laying on the floor of the cab between our seats. Everything in the bag has melted, sunscreen, lip balm, deodorant, etc. It truly was a hot journey across the desert.

We feel a whole lot better after a shower and Domino's pizza in our room.

After dinner, I call my childhood friend, Rick. We grew up in the same neighborhood and our families camped together on Campers Island in Hustisford, Wisconsin, for many years. Rick now lives in Riverside, California, and has offered to host us for a couple of days upon completion of our trip. I let him know we made it to California, and that we should be to Santa Monica in a couple of days. He assures me he will be there to pick us up. I am excited to see Rick as it has been way too long.

Tomorrow, we will return the U-Haul and continue by bicycle toward Santa Monica Pier and the Pacific Ocean. We are excited for the next two days (eighty miles) of our adventure, which should see us through to the end of Route 66.

Facebook followers

Cathy Skott
Smart move on the truck. You guys are awesome, enjoy your successes. I finished the East Coast Greenway. Going for the proof picture now!

Molly French
Very good call on the truck! I think you've biked plenty.) Enjoy the last 80 miles, although I am sad your posts will be ending. Really look forward to following your adventures.

Dawn N Hal Goodman
Also agree the truck was the way to go. Better safe than sorry.

Santa Monica, California, and its famous pier marks the end point of historic Route 66 as well as the last of our three cross-country bicycle adventures.

Chapter 9

State of California

July 20-21, 2016
89 miles/2,603 total

Day 48
July 20 – San Bernardino to Arcadia, California
50 miles (total miles – 2,564)
Sunny, 98 degrees, slight headwind

Tracy

We wake up in California. Yea! Our first task is to return the U-Haul truck we used to drive across the desert yesterday. Thanks to my good planning, our return site is only 2.7 miles away from our hotel and one block off route. After breakfast in our room (oatmeal again), we pack our bags, put them back in the truck, and drive to the return site. Once there, we pull everything back out, check in the truck, load the bicycle, and head west.

About the Mojave Desert

"The Mojave Desert occupies a significant portion of Southern California and parts of Utah, Nevada, and Arizona. Named after the Mojave Native Americans, it occupies roughly 54,000 square miles in a typical Basin and Range topography. The Mojave Desert receives less than 6 inches of rain a year and is generally between 3,000 and 6,000 feet in elevation. The Mojave Desert also contains the Mojave National Preserve, Joshua Tree National Park and the lowest-hottest place in North America: Death Valley, where the temperature can approach 120 in late July and early August. High winds, often above 50 miles per hour, are also a weather factor and occur frequently along the western end of the Mojave and are less common toward the east."
https://mojavedesert.net/

Arcadia, California, is by no means in the middle of nowhere, yet this suburban Los Angeles community still embraces its Route 66 heritage as evidenced by the signage on this overpass that Tracy is viewing from close up.

We arrive at the Pacific Electric Inland Empire Trail eight miles into the ride. For the next eighteen miles, we ride on one of the best trails we have ever been on. It is a beautiful and traffic-free way to get through the Los Angeles suburbs. The trail takes us through cities, orange groves, rose gardens, residential, and commercial/industrial areas. We are also starting to see lots of palm trees and Joshua trees.

It is fun to see the different types of trees and flowers. The trail is well-designed with many intersection crossings. The crossings are amazing, with priority push button signals for the smaller road intersections, while the major road crossings typically bring the trail to the closest signalized intersection. Interestingly, they have separate push buttons at the intersections for walkers, bicyclists, and even horseback riders (their buttons are up high so they can reach them from horseback).

Peter

Once we leave the trail, we are traveling on city streets with great bicycle accommodations. Most of the roads are wide, smooth and/or have bicycle lanes. We have plenty of space on the busier streets. California seems to do a good job of building its roads for all users. It is really nice to see.

The only issue we must deal with today is the heat. This is the hottest day of the trip so far. When we reach Arcadia at 3 p.m., the temperature is a scorching 98 degrees. By taking our time and staying hydrated, we have handled the heat well. I think at this point we are finally acclimated, although we are definitely looking forward to a shower and an air-conditioned hotel room.

Searching the internet for a hotel room with my phone, we discover there is only one room left in town tonight for some reason. (Almost homeless again.) The Hilton Garden Inn it will be. We had not intended to go quite this high end ($219), but after fifty miles in these temperatures and on our last night of the trip, $219 doesn't seem that bad.

Tomorrow is a red-letter day! We are only thirty miles from Santa Monica Pier and the end of our bicycle adventure along Route 66. We have enjoyed the trip, but it has been a lot of work. We will be glad to be done. Our friend, Rick, will pick us up between 2 and 3 p.m. We cannot wait to get started in the morning!

Day 49
July 21 – Arcadia to Santa Monica, California
39 miles (total miles – 2,603)
Sunny, 90 degrees, light wind

Tracy

After breakfast in our room, we pack our bags and load the bike for the last time.

As it turned out, our room last night was not as expensive as we thought it would be. It was free! Unfortunately/fortunately, my side of our fancy adjustable bed was broken, and management comped our room. (Peter was appreciative of me taking one for the team.)

We are on the road by 8 a.m. on this Thursday morning. We have plenty of time to make it to Santa Monica, look around, savor the end of the trip, and meet Rick for a ride to his house in Riverside.

Our Adventure Cycling map warns us about bicycling to Santa Monica: "Expect urban riding conditions from San Bernardino to Santa Monica, with increasing traffic levels as you head west. Riding miles from Pasadena to Santa Monica on an early Sunday morning can help also. The route ends at the Santa Monica Pier on the Pacific Ocean."

Peter

Our hope this morning was to time traffic so we could catch the break between the morning and the noon rushes. Not! What break? This is doable, but it definitely is urban riding. Between the traffic, frequent stops and starts (the tandem, especially fully loaded, isn't really designed for heavy city traffic), heat, and our gen-

Exploring the Hollywood Walk of Fame while guiding the tandem through crowds of tourists seemed like a good idea at the time. Maybe not so much.

eral fatigue from forty-nine days on the road, this is tough.

On the recommendation of our guidebook, we decide to go off route .3 miles and check out the famous Hollywood Walk of Fame, twenty miles into the ride. This seemed like a good idea at the time, but what we missed was the word "walk." There are thousands of tourists, just like us, wandering among the stars. It is impossible to ride the tandem in this crowd, so we dismount. But it is even difficult for us to pick our way through the crowd on foot. Ultimately, Tracy takes the lead and I follow pushing the bike. While we do "see" the Walk of Fame, we do not recommend pushing a fully loaded tandem down this particular sidewalk, at noon, during peak tourist season. Ha! Live and learn. We do not stay long and are soon on the road again.

About seven miles from the end of the ride, our rear tire starts to "feel funny." Surely it will make it another seven miles! Then it starts to feel REALLY funny.

"Stop! Stop! STOP!" Tracy yells.

We pull to the side of the road, right in front of a Starbucks. After a bit of investigation, we discover that the sidewall of the tire is in the process of failing! We knew the tire was on its last legs, but thought we could limp it in. Nope! After unloading the tent and rear panniers, replacing the spent tire with a brand new one, and reloading everything one more time, we continue on our way.

We have a great ride through Beverly Hills with its amazing homes and Rodeo Drive, where I have to keep reminding Tracy that we are not here to shop. We drop down to Sunset Boulevard and then Broadway. The ride along Broadway is very nice with a bicycle lane and slower-moving traffic. We can feel the temperature drop as we travel west, then we smell the ocean, and finally, we can see it. Left on Ocean Avenue, one block and we are there. Santa Monica Pier!

We have traveled 2,603 miles in forty-nine days, unsupported, on a tandem bicycle named "Violet." Wow! We did it. Who gets to do this!

I reach my hand back to Tracy and she grabs it and gives it a squeeze. "Where do you want to go next?" I ask.

"I don't know for sure," she replies, "But I do know I want to ride the rest of the states."

"I'm in!" I say.

I know she is smiling and crying close behind me.

Tracy

I am always emotional at the end of our trips, crying, and yes, at the same time smiling. I have mixed feelings. I am happy about the successful trip and all the adventures we had, and I'm glad it is over. However, I'm also sad to see it come to an end. I don't know, I guess I am just a mess!

Because of our slow progress through the city traffic and the tire issue, our time at the Santa Monica Pier is way too brief. We only have forty-five minutes until Rick arrives. We do two quick phone interviews overlooking

We get teary-eyed overlooking the Santa Monica Pier behind Tracy. The end of a journey of this magnitude generates mixed emotions for both of us.

the pier, one with Steve Horrell, reporter for the *Edwardsville (IL) Intelligencer* and the other with Cassandra Duvall, NBC26 TV anchor from our hometown, Green Bay. We then head to the pier itself for the obligatory photo ops with the "Santa Monica, Yacht Harbor, Sport Fishing, Boating, Cafes" entrance sign and "Santa Monica 66 End of the Trail" sign. It is difficult to get the photos because there are so many people trying to do the same thing. There is actually a line of people waiting to get a picture of the trail sign. We patiently wait in line, but at the same time I am thinking, "I bet none of you bicycled all the way here from Green Bay, Wisconsin. My turn!"

Finally, we head to the Bike Center on 2nd Street to meet Rick. He lives in Riverside about ninety miles away, but is in Santa Monica on business and had agreed to pick us up. Right on time, we see Rick's white pickup truck pull into the small parking lot. We load the bicycle into the truck and we are on our way. We made it!

We will spend the next couple of days with Rick at his house, recovering and relaxing before heading home.

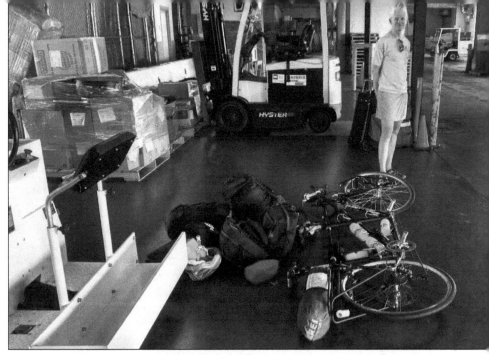

We nervously wait with our tandem in the hopes there are no issues getting it accepted for transport aboard Amtrak for our trip back to Wisconsin.

Epilogue

Recovery Day 1
(July 22, 2016)

Peter

We wake up at our friend Rick's house in Riverside, California, and have nowhere to go. Rick has a beautiful home and has agreed to let us stay, rest, and relax for the next four days. From here, we will take the Amtrak Southwest Chief passenger train to Milwaukee, Wisconsin, followed by a two-hour car ride home courtesy of Tracy's dad.

We learned after our 2014 Northern Tier cross-country bicycle trip not to drive home if we can avoid it. (See our book, *Coast to Coast on a Tandem*.) Being confined to a mid-size car going 75 mph, with the bike in pieces in the back, after having traveled under our own power at bicycle speeds for seventy-two days, was downright disturbing. We took the train from New Orleans to Milwaukee after our Mississippi River trip the following year and found it to be much more relaxing. The constant motion of the train, privacy of our sleeper car, the ability to walk and stretch our legs, explore the train, and enjoy the spectacular meals in the dining car made it a memorable experience and a wonderful way to return to "normal" life. There is definitely a sense of culture shock after a long bicycle trip. Everything is so loud and moves so fast.

Rick has to work today, so we have the entire house to ourselves except for Rick's German Shepherd, Lucy, who is a love and a wonderful therapy dog. Rick later said we spoiled her.

We go out to dinner with Rick at Tios Tacos, a quirky eatery on Mission Avenue featuring Mexican cuisine. After dinner, we explore the historic Mission Inn and Spa. Rick knows a secret way in.

Recovery Day 2
(July 23, 2016)

Our muscles are sore and we are very tired today. Inevitably, trip fatigue kicks in two to three days after a major bicycle

Mission Inn Hotel & Spa

"Originally built as a two-story adobe guesthouse in 1876, the Mission Inn Hotel & Spa has become the crown jewel of Southern California. This National Historic Landmark allows guests to experience the enchantment of a European castle with the Inn's one-of-a-kind architecture. The hotel is also a California State Landmark and the heart of Riverside. Kelly's Spa was ranked among the top ten on Condé Nast Traveler's "Top 50 Hotel Spas in the United States." The Mission Inn Hotel & Spa Festival of Lights was also ranked as the "Best Public Lights Display" in the 2018 USA Today 10 Best Readers' Choice Awards, received Historic Hotels "Best Social Media of a Historic Hotel" in 2018, named "Best Historic Hotel" in the 2017 USA Today 10 Best Readers' Choice Awards. From its grand archways and iconic domes to its 20,000 sq. ft. of function space for events and weddings, the AAA Four Diamond Mission Inn Hotel & Spa offers a luxurious experience with each stay." https://www.historichotels.org/us/hotels-resorts/the-mission-inn-hotel-and-spa/?

adventure. We rest and relax with Lucy while Rick works. Television has not gotten any better in our absence, and apparently, the world has not come to an end. While we are definitely moving slowly, we are ready to head out for dinner and a drink by the time Rick gets home from work.

Facebook followers

Peter Flucke is with Tracy Flucke at Heroes Restaurant & Brewery.
July 23, 2016

Tom Walsh
Can never have too much recovery.

Rebecca Cleveland
Well deserved.

Paul Knickelbine
So well deserved!

Christine Healey
That's an important part of a proper recovery!

Collette LaRue
The best part?

Peter Flucke
Nope! Imagine, plan, train, experience, recover, remember, share. They are all equally the best part - in due time.

Wayne Paider
BIG smiles. It's over. Congrats.

Dawn N Hal Goodman
Lookin' good!

David Paider
I can't tell the difference, every stop you made on the tour was at a pub!

Recovery Day 3
(July 24, 2016)

It is Sunday and Rick drives us the sixty-five miles to Huntington Beach. We really enjoy walking in the sand, dipping our toes in the ocean, and people watching. We are still bummed we could not spend more time at Santa Monica Pier and this helps. An extra treat was watching the Vans US Open of Surfing (WSL) competition. The surf was definitely up.

Facebook followers

Peter Flucke is with Tracy Flucke at Huntington Beach Pier.
July 24, 2016, Huntington Beach, California

Dale Nimmo
You lazy bums!

Peter Flucke
80/20 Dale Nimmo, 80/20.

Tracy and Peter Flucke

Paul Knickelbine
So glad to see you guys relaxing.
Order some Thai delivered.

Wayne Paider
Bet it is nice to be off that bike seat.

Al Pahnke
You guys ROCK!

Dawn N Hal Goodman
We've been on that pier. Nice place
to be by the sea.

Ann Evans Dettlaff
You actually look like tourists
(except for the white feet).

Paul Knickelbine
Manhattan beach, rent a boogie
board, my fav.

Our friend, Rick, took us down to the ocean at Huntington Beach Pier for a much-appreciated day of relaxation.

Recovery Day 4
(July 25, 2016)

Today is very chill. We snuggle with Lucy in the morning, and I get a haircut and shave in the afternoon. In the evening, I change one final flat tire. Seriously, it went flat in the garage. I then remove the pedals from the bike in preparation for boxing it up tomorrow at the Amtrak station.

Recovery Day 5
(July 26, 2016)

It is time to start our journey home. We have the bike and our gear loaded by 9 a.m. and secured into the back of Rick's pickup truck for the fifty-five-mile drive to Union Station in Los Angeles. Traffic, as always, is heavy, but by 11 a.m. we are standing on the train loading dock with the bike.

Tracy purchased our tickets earlier in the week. We are traveling in style and have a two-person roomette in the sleeper car.

Now comes the tricky part. Amtrak does accept bicycles as baggage, but "NO non-standard bicycles" (aka tandems), according to its website. Standard bicycles must be packed in a bike box purchased from Amtrak ($10.) Once the bike's pedals and handlebars are removed, and the box is taped shut, you are good to go. There is usually a bit of extra space in the box for spare gear. It is a pretty slick system. Some trains now have baggage cars specially equipped with bicycle racks which allow "standard" bikes to simply be rolled on and off.

So what to do with the tandem? The word on the street is that "unofficially," Amtrak will allow you to "double box" a tandem, telescope two boxes together, and ship it that way. This is exactly what we did from New Orleans to Milwaukee after our Mississippi River trip last year. The only hitch is that you need a friendly baggage handler or the gig may be up. If this happens, we have three backup plans. Plan A is to try and find a friendlier baggage handler. Plan B is to take the bike apart using the S&S couplers, pad the heck out of it, and put it in a single bike box. It might fit, but we would never want to do this because the bike likely would get destroyed. Plan C is to simply stay here in California. We are not going anywhere without this bike!

Fortunately, on our first try, we find a very friendly baggage handler. At first, he looks at our bike with concern. But when I say (with a great deal of confidence), "I usually just double box it," he replies, "That'll work." By 11:40 a.m., the bike is boxed and we are free to explore LA until we board the 6:10 p.m. Amtrak Southwest Chief to Chicago.

Before we left for our trip, one of our daughter Alex's high school classmates reached out to us to say he would be in LA for the summer, and it would be great to see us at the end of our trip. At 3:30 p.m. we meet Austin in the rotunda of Union Station. It is so good to see a friendly face from back home. We go for a short walk, get something to eat, and are back at the station by 4:30 p.m.

Facebook followers

Peter Flucke is with Tracy Flucke at Union Station Los Angeles.
July 26, 2016, Los Angeles, California

The bike is boxed and ready to go with us on the 6:10 p.m. Amtrak Southwest Chief!

Katie Hafsoos Commer
Another great adventure! When is the next one?

Peter Flucke
Please stand by!

Tracy and Peter Flucke

Tim Bauknecht
Sending it to the Smithsonian for display?

Peter Flucke
Right! It or us. Lol

Janet Roberts
Well, that answers my question about how you're getting the bike back home. Have a safe and interesting trip.

Dale Nimmo
MONGO box!

Tracy Flucke
Remember it is a tandem Dale!

Dennis Wiechmann (Peter's cousin)
Safe travels! Bummed we could not work out seeing you! Wisconsin it is! Or maybe Bellingham!

Peter Flucke
We will be in Vancouver, BC, for the International Pro Walk, Pro Bike, Pro Place Conf. Sept 12-15 (with stops in Bellingham) maybe around then - if you are not too busy with school. Hope David is feeling better soon!

Thomas Florack
See you soon. When do you get in Friday? And where?

Peter Flucke
Tracy's parents will be bringing us home from Milwaukee either Thursday night or sometime on Friday.

Thomas Florack
Enjoy the ride back!

Rebecca Cleveland
Mission accomplished!

Dick Schaffer
What a great way to travel! On my bucket list!

Peter Flucke
Do it! It's a great way to travel if you have the time.

Peter Flucke is with Tracy Flucke and Austin Kadulski at Union Station Los Angeles. July 26, 2016, Los Angeles, California

So good to see a friendly face today in LA. Thanks for coming down to see us off, Austin Kadulski.

Alexandra Flucke (daughter extraordinare #2)
Lol how did this happen?

We enjoyed our ride on Amtrak back to Wisconsin.

Peter Flucke
Austin has been working in LA all summer. He reached out to us before the trip and we finally were able to get together. Great guy!

Recovery Day 6
(July 27, 2016)

Peter Flucke
July 27, 2016

Currently retracing our We Bike Route 66 adventure via Amtrak somewhere in New Mexico.

Steve Wexler
Hopefully a bit more relaxing on the way back.

Peter Flucke
Just a different kind of relaxing Steve.

Recovery Day 7
(July 28, 2016)

Peter Flucke is in Amtrak, Naperville, Illinois.
July 28, 2016

We made a new friend on the train from Los Angeles to Chicago. Almost to the Windy City.

Paula Roberts
Awww!

Barb Erb
Nice. Never thought about taking my dog cross country on a train.

Julie Brainard Nelsen
Cute friend!

Ian Rousseau
Now you are going to need a 3 seat tandem bike - or get a basket for handlebars (a big basket)!

Peter Flucke
Lol

Darlene Luedtke Charles
Awe Nice! We had a white German Shepherd back in the day...Lancer, was his name.

Peter Flucke
This was a great dog. I actually miss him.

Darlene Luedtke Charles
Maybe he was your guardian angel dog.

We had a visitor spend some time with us on the train.

Peter Flucke is traveling to Green Bay, Wisconsin, from Union Station - Amtrak Trains.
July 28, 2016, Chicago, Illinois

Getting closer!

Bob Healey
Going to be back the last Thursday, Friday in August...so if you are around.

Peter Flucke
Cool! Let us know if you need a place to stay.

Peter Flucke
July 28, 2016

Well, we made it to Milwaukee. Unfortunately, our bike and two of our bags won't be here until 9:40 p.m. tonight. Spending the night with Tracy's parents in Wauwatosa and then heading home to Ashwaubenon (Green Bay) in the morning. Just a little more adventure.

Greg Cribb (baggage manager for Delta Airlines)
How do bags get lost on a train? Lol. Didn't this happen before?

Peter Flucke
Well, technically, not lost, just oversized. Our train didn't have a baggage car. BTW, how do bags get lost on planes? Lol. Yup, this happened last fall on our way back from New Orleans.

Greg Cribb
Most airlines loose one bag per 10k. I just envision a lone train car with the bags sitting in the middle of nowhere. lol

Peter Flucke
Me too!

Toni Osterberg
That was a quick bike ride back to Wisconsin! lol

We finally have our tandem and gear in hand and ready for the drive to Green Bay, courtesy of Tracy's dad.

Peter Schleinz
We must have just missed you! We are in MKE tonight and flying out in the morning.

Peter Flucke
Where are you going?

Peter Schleinz
Boston and Ptown for a long weekend.
Leaving all automobile options behind on this trip.

Jessika Meisner (our niece)
Stop in Waukesha!

Peter Flucke
Love you guys but too tired this time. Come to Green Bay. Lol See you soon!

Jessika Meisner
lol Tell us when! lol

Laura Holly
Well, welcome back to Wisconsin!

Cleva Bickford
Glad you are home safe.

Home!
(July 29, 2016)

Peter Flucke is with Tracy Flucke.
July 29, 2016

Well, it took twelve hours longer than we expected but, the bike is loaded and we are on our way HOME! ETA Green Bay: 2:40 p.m.

Lynne Dzuba
Excited to have you back +all the tales.

Patrick Wondrash (Tracy's cousin)
Who's that old guy by the van? Lol

Peter Flucke
And we are HOME!
Looking forward to catching up with our old friends and missing all of our new friends already! Thanks again to ALL of you for your support during this adventure!

It always feels great to be home after one of our cross-country trips. We have just arrived in this photo, as evidenced by the non-riding condition of our tandem and the borrowed clothes we're wearing from Tracy's parents.

Julie Brainard Nelsen
Welcome home!

Christian Jensen
About time! Now...go cut your grass. Welcome home.

Katie Hafsoos Commer
Another awesome journey! Welcome home!

Kathy Crain Wondrash
Welcome home.

Toni Osterberg
Welcome home...glad you made it home safely.

Mary Ebeling
We want to get up to GB to see you sometime before the end times!

Peter Flucke
You are always welcome. There is some fun stuff to do here. No, really!

John Z Wetmore
How soon do you have to leave to cycle across Canada for ProWalk/ProBike/Pro-Place in Vancouver in September?

Kerry Janquart
You two are amazing!

Helen Marcks
Welcome home!

Lee Hyrkas (our nutritionist)
Welcome home! Glad you guys made it safe and sound!

Cathy Skott
Welcome home, glad you are back safely!

Patrick Wondrash
Welcome back!

Christine Williquette
See you soon?!

Darlene Luedtke Charles
Welcome back home...Do we get to see you sitting in your Lazy Boys now?

Peter Flucke
Maybe for a week or two.

Bob Blihar
Welcome home!

Edward Lin
Another successful ride. Congrats and welcome back home!

Christine Healey
Yay!

Mark Leland
Great job you two! Welcome home!

***

2017

We decided to take a break from major bicycle touring in 2017. With three cross-country trips and over 10,000 miles under our belts (2014 -Northern

Tier, 4,362 miles, 2015 - Mississippi River, 3,052 miles, 2016 – Route 66, 2,603 miles) and with our daughter, Melissa, getting married in June, we thought it was time. We planned to be back at it in 2018.

2018

Tracy was hit by a car in July of 2018 while riding her bicycle on a quiet Sunday morning, only three miles from our home. A motorist coming from Tracy's right blew a stop sign and then failed to yield the right of way. Even with all her training and experience, there was nothing Tracy could do. Concussion, whiplash, bruising, and a knee that would require surgery were the result. Following surgery to repair a complex tear of her medial meniscus and rehab, she was cleared by her doctor to train and tour again. So, we started to train for our most ambitious tour yet.

2019

Our last major bicycle tour, Sierra and Cascade Mountains (1,456 miles, 34 days) was in 2019. Our plan going into the trip was to bicycle approximately 7,000 miles in five months and ride through the twenty-one states in the lower forty-eight we had not biked yet. Unfortunately, the extremes of the trip, which was one of our most difficult, proved to be too much for Tracy physically and mentally, and for us as a tandem team. Live to fight another day.

2020

In January of 2020, the Department of Health and Human Services declared the Novel Coronavirus (2019-nCoV) outbreak a public health emergency. We were still able to bike and took advantage of the freedom to get out, but few services were open or available. We handled the lack of services well. I guess all those bicycle touring miles with "limited or no services" prepared us for the pandemic.

Tracy was appointed to the Ashwaubenon Village Board in October and assigned to chair the Bicycle and Pedestrian Committee. She had founded this committee as the parks and recreation director more than twenty years earlier.

2021

Tracy won election to the Ashwaubenon Village Board in April of 2021 and continued to chair the Bicycle and Pedestrian Committee.

In August, after over twenty years and more than 60,000 miles of riding Violet, Tracy finally allowed me to buy a new tandem. What convinced her was me pointing out that if the new bike lasted for twenty years, like Violet did, we would be eighty when it was "time for a new tandem." (https://we-bikeetc.wordpress.com/2021/08/)

Our new bicycle ("The Dream Machine") is a 2020 Co-Motion Speedster Co-Pilot with a 14-speed internal Rohloff speedhub and belt drive.

2022

I was invited to speak at the 27th Annual Kansas Transportation Safety Conference in Topeka in early April of 2022, and we were thrilled. This presented an opportunity for another serious ride and to check a few more boxes on our "to ride" list.

We left Green Bay April 3 and drove our minivan, with the Dream Machine inside, to Topeka for the conference. We abandoned the minivan in the conference hotel parking lot three days later, loaded the tandem, and headed out for a month-long, unsupported ride that would cover approximately 1,200 miles. Generally, our route was to be Topeka, Kansas – Kearney, Nebraska – Cheyenne, Wyoming – Denver, Colorado – Topeka, Kansas.

We chose this route because I have relatives who came across the country by covered wagon on the Oregon Trail in 1850 and 1862. Our route would follow almost 500 miles of the 1862 route from Topeka to western Nebraska.

Unfortunately, the weather that spring was exceptionally bad, even for Kansas and Nebraska. Winds were often sustained at 30 mph with gusts topping 50 mph. The wind chill one day fell to just 11 degrees. Surprisingly, we had a really good time. Tracy's knee was strong, the new bike was a dream to ride, the roads were generally low trafficked, motorists polite, and the people we met wonderful. We were actually able to ride in these conditions if the wind direction was just right.

At one point, though, I had to point the tandem into the wind while stopped just so I could hold it steady enough for Tracy to get back on. Epic! Ultimately, we just could not make enough progress to meet our timeline and had to end the trip after "just" 400 miles. We rented another ten-foot U-Haul truck in Kearney, Nebraska, and drove back to Topeka.

***

Looking back on our 2019 and 2022 tour attempts, we were somewhat surprised that we had to abandon them. When we started doing cross-country bicycle tours at the ages of fifty-plus, we knew that, someday, we would not be able to long-tour anymore. But, after more than 10,000 miles of successful cross-country touring, we had almost started to take our success for granted. No longer! What we have been able to do is a privilege, surpassed possibly only by the privilege of sharing our experiences with others. Neither are to be taken for granted.

***

2023 and beyond

We are not sure what the future will bring but, hopefully, we will see you on the road!

Acknowledgements

Our cross-country bicycle trip along historic Route 66 was a challenge, as was completing this book about our epic journey. Both endeavors required the support of many.

We knew writing a book was daunting from our experience writing our first book, *Coast to Coast on a Tandem,* and that a good editor/publisher was a must. When we were contemplating writing this book, we again reached out to Mike Dauplaise and Bonnie Groessl of M&B Global Solutions Inc., only to learn they had retired from the book-writing gig. Bummer!

When we finally made the decision to write this book, we asked Mike and Bonnie for suggestions on a new editor/publisher. We were excited when Mike told us they had decided to take on book projects again and would help with our new book. We now had a great team and knew we would be successful. We truly value their professionalism, expertise, and friendship.

Just like our first book, this book includes many Facebook and blog comments from our followers. Their support during our trip was invaluable, helping us through the tough times and making the good times even sweeter. Thank you to all who followed us and provided likes, loves, smiles, and comments.

Finally, special thanks to the active supporters of Route 66 for all your hard work keeping this amazing corridor the special and historic place it is.

Ride on!

Tracy and Peter Flucke (Summer 2023)